# super tonics

# super tonics

### 75 Adaptogen-Packed Recipes to Boost Immunity, Sleep, Beauty, and Wellness

Meredith Youngson

Photography by Jocelynne Flor

TEN SPEED PRESS
California | New York

This book is dedicated to my husband, Peter.
I'm sorry for the Golden Mylk stains I left in your car.

# contents

## golden hour   127

## beauty sleep   159

## superfood staples   179

## closing gratitude   186
## index   188

# preface

It all began in 2011 with a blueberry-almond smoothie and a fifteen-dollar blender—one of those handheld immersion kinds most people use for soup. I had the idea to combine almond milk, frozen blueberries, and oats to create a healthy beverage that would energize my tired college-student brain. This simple act of self-care was revelatory to me in that moment.

At twenty-one, I was overwhelmed, insecure, and uninspired by the path I was on. I was struggling to keep up with my demanding college program, and my yearslong battle with chronic dieting and disordered eating was taking its toll on my mental and physical health.

As a tween growing up in the 1990s, body-positivity leaders, mental wellness advocates, and proud feminists weren't celebrated in the media like they are today. I worshipped *Seventeen* and *Cosmo* magazines for teaching me how to do a smoky eye, and I browsed "skinny girl" Tumblr accounts to learn all the ways to get by on less food.

Luckily, by 2011, conversations around food were moving from "low calorie" and "portion control" to "vibrant, nutrient-dense whole foods," and I discovered the amazing world of healthy food blogs. Inspiring, trailblazing women behind websites like *Oh She Glows*, *My New Roots*, *The First Mess*, *Ambitious Kitchen*, and *This Rawsome Vegan Life* weren't telling us how to lose weight—they were celebrating delicious, feel-good food and the joy of being in the kitchen. This was life-changing to me. This sparked my own Oprah "aha" moment to start recognizing food as fuel, fun, and nourishment rather than a means for punishment and control.

In my own kitchen, where I had little experience (besides the sandwich skills my roommates loved me for), I wanted to teach myself everything about healthy eating and cooking. I pumped buckwheat banana bread, lentil meatballs, quinoa granola, spirulina smoothies, and spiralized noodles out of my kitchen daily. I traded my calorie tracker for a plant-based diet and kept my bowl full of dark leafy greens. With plenty of energy and a new lease on life, I just had to share this passion with others (or at least show off my awesome super-seed cookie recipe). With that, my first food blog—*Peachy Clean Eats*—was born. Through the twists and turns of my early twenties, creating and sharing these recipes was my hobby—and escape—from the underlying anxiety and low self-esteem I was struggling with.

Wanting to make my love of nutrition "official," in 2014 I went back to the books to become a registered holistic nutritionist in Toronto. I wholeheartedly soaked up my nutrition studies while sharing my healthy living tips and recipes on my blog and Instagram. Back then, the plant-based online community was small but supportive, and I enthusiastically posted my daily green smoothie bowl or lentil salad. Solidifying my passion for plants, I worked alongside an incredible raw food chef, Barbara Maccaroni, as she opened her restaurant B.Love Conscious Eatery, which served up some of the first raw vegan food Hamilton, Ontario, had to offer. Through watching Barbara make her creations (and tasting them!), I learned just how beautiful, flavorful, and gratifying plant-based food could be.

My hard work churning out recipes paid off in 2016, when I landed my dream job developing recipes for a leading meal kit company. In this role I was able to learn how to complement my plant-based recipe approach with classic flavor pairings and cooking techniques. I learned all I could from my talented, professionally trained chef colleagues and tested hundreds of recipes a year that made it to hundreds of thousands of plates. However, my mental health struggles were far from over, and the stress from starting a new job turned my anxiety and depression up to full volume.

I pulled away from friends and was terrified of Mondays, and spontaneous fits of tears were the norm. I felt broken—like something was wrong with me and needed fixing. I either had to quit my dream job and move back home with my parents to feel "safe" again, or I had to get better.

So I decided to try to get better. I started seeing a therapist, listened to TED Talks and read Brené Brown books in the tub, went on long walks with inspirational podcasts, took manifestation courses, and borrowed dozens of self-development books from the library. After months of absorbing these positive sources of brain food, I was able to develop a healthy perspective and the coping skills to help manage my day-to-day anxiety. I focused on self-compassion over perfection. I was inspired to work toward living an amazing—not just safe—life.

Feeling all the benefits of these self-care techniques, I started considering how our diets and our thoughts around food impact our mental health. It hurt me to realize this, but I eventually came to terms with the fact that my "peachy clean" vegan diet was just another sneaky method of control and restriction. After (painfully) ripping off the vegan label and slowly letting go of the shame behind "good" and "bad" foods, I completely opened up the gates of my diet and began eating intuitively. I continued to enjoy the delicious plant foods I loved (and still do) but without the title of Super Healthy Vegan Girl. I fried eggs in butter, consumed white sugar without cringing, and attended parties without packing my own protein bar. It felt incredibly freeing and allowed me to fully explore my love affair with food. I reevaluated my mission and mantra and created my current food blog—*Earth & Oven*—which celebrates my passion for exploring the intersection of plant-based nutrition, wellness, flavor, fun, and decadence.

As a part of my eating-for-joy adventure, I began researching different foods that promote happiness and reduce stress, and that led me to the power of herbs, teas, and tonics. Could an all-natural herbal tea also work as an anxiety aid? It sounded amazing to this plant-loving nutritionist. So I began experimenting with tea blends to bolster my anxiety-busting toolbox. Being a foodie and cook, it was important to me that the blends were as delicious as they were functional. There were enough teas out there that tasted like grass—no thank you.

Through my passion to empower myself to feel better and help others do the same, my organic wellness tea company Lake & Oak Tea Co. was born. Inspired by the amazing effects of that tea, I got to work creating functional tea blends for skin health, detox, digestion, inflammation, and stress.

Lake & Oak Tea Co. launched quietly on Christmas Eve in 2017, when I stickered a handful of pouches at home and handed them out to relatives as gifts the next day. A roller-coaster ride of entrepreneurship later, Lake & Oak now has more than twenty signature Superfood Teas and Latte Blends available at hundreds of health and eco-conscious retailers in North America. Through the years, Lake & Oak has grown and evolved and found its voice in a crowded category.

Tea, and other beverages we drink, are highly personal; they are a part of our daily routines and lives, good or bad. I am grateful to be a positive part of someone's day, that first sip of green tea you take in the morning to wake up or the last sip of chamomile at the end of the day when you're curled up in bed. Hearing from our lovely customers that our tea is their "healthy obsession that feels like a treat" or their "favorite evening ritual" pushes me to continue to create healthy and delicious teas to make someone's day.

With that love for life-giving beverages, self-care, and sharing delicious things with others, I present to you this book: *Super Tonics*.

Cheers to you, wherever you are on this wild journey.

*Meredith*

# introduction

Before we dig into all things tonics, let's get on the same page about the terms *tonic* and *elixir*. In this book, I use them interchangeably to describe nourishing, feel-good beverages.

Some dictionary definitions of the word *tonic* are "a medicinal substance taken to give a feeling of vigor or well-being" and "anything invigorating physically, mentally, or morally."

*Elixir,* on the other hand, is defined as "a particular type of medicinal solution."

## Spilling the Tea on Tonics

Whether you are calling them tonics, elixirs, drinks, or magical potions, the recipes in this book are formulated with ingredients and techniques to taste delicious, make you feel amazing, and provide both instant and long-term benefits. You'll notice from the pretty array of glassware that we are focusing on beneficial beverages in the form of teas, lattes, plant milks, smoothies, infusions, and hydrating elixirs. To complement the delicious wellness drinks, you'll also find recipes for nourishing soups, grain bowls, salads, and power snacks to fuel your day.

The book is organized into sections by time of day, with tonics that will complement your daily rituals and patterns, whether it's your hectic morning commute (Get Up & Glow, page 53), your 3:00 p.m. slump (Good Vibes All Day, page 95), your evening chill time (Golden Hour, page 127), or getting ready for bed (Beauty Sleep, page 159).

## Tonics & Self-Care

I believe there is a tonic to elevate every mood, lifestyle, or time of day. Whether you are juggling two jobs, starting a business, training for a marathon, or simply looking for more time to care for yourself, this book has a tonic to support you.

You'll find everything from recipes that take thirty seconds to whip up as you are heading out the door (like the Love Your Guts Spritzer, page 133) to others that involve a bit more time and patience to create (such as the Tulsi-Lavender Lemonade, page 163).

Alongside all the tasty elixirs, you'll find some of my tried-and-trusted tips for self-care, mental health, and mindset sprinkled throughout the book. I like to think of tonics and self-care tools as puzzle pieces that fit together as part of our overall health and wellness.

In my own life and wellness routine, daily tonics are a consistent, grounding ritual that I use to help energize, de-stress, inspire, or ground myself. Whatever might be going on in my day, I look forward to taking care of my mind and body with a tonic.

My morning digestive tonic is more than a recipe; it also represents a time to slow down, check in with myself, and reflect. My daily Super Coffee (page 62) is loaded with things that prepare me mentally for whatever the day brings. The evening tonic I prepare—Chamomile Serenity CBD Latte (page 167)—helps me celebrate the little things (like getting through Monday!). As I sip slowly, my drink reminds me to connect to a more restful state and prepare for bedtime.

Life can move fast, and we tend to focus on the "doing" part of existence rather than the "being." Taking these moments throughout the day for yourself is an act of self-love that can bring positive impacts to every aspect of your life.

## Why You Should Care About Self-Care

Self-care isn't selfish. I remind myself of this when pangs of guilt set in for taking the afternoon off work for a mental health date, for clearing my weekend for some me time, or for stacking my bookshelf with personal development books.

Self-care belongs to everyone. Marketing and social media can have us believing that taking care of ourselves means splurging on a vacation or indulging in an expensive smoothie bowl. But my most satisfying days of self-care don't involve time at the spa; rather, the satisfaction comes after setting boundaries in my relationships or doing little things that positively impact my mental health (like taking a walk in nature or having a phone-free evening).

My passion for self-care is rooted in the experiences I've had and the lessons I've learned on my mental health journey. As a young adult, the anxiety and depression I was struggling with for the first time left me feeling alienated, embarrassed, and unworthy. After reaching out to a therapist and speaking openly with friends and family, I began to explore ways I could feel empowered in my mental health and wellness. Developing a self-care routine has had a profound effect on my life, and yet, the journey isn't over; in fact, it's ever-evolving. Over the past decade I've built a toolbox of self-care practices that I refer to daily. To learn more about these tools, see Five-Minute Self-Care Practices (page 16). I also begin each chapter by offering ways you can incorporate self-care into your day. For now, here are more reasons to prioritize self-care.

## Self-Care Is Good for Your Health

In addition to the more obvious mental health benefits, our level of self-care can have an impact on our physical well-being. With stress being connected to so many illnesses, partaking in activities that benefit your mental and physical wellness can support everything from your immunity and energy levels to your digestion, sleep, and skin.

## Self-Care Is Good for Relationships

I know firsthand the impact that unchecked anxiety and overwhelm can have on a relationship. I used to pick fights and set unreachable expectations with my husband because of the turbulence I was experiencing internally. When I began to face my feelings and develop self-awareness, I became a better partner, daughter, sister, and friend.

On the flip side, it is incredibly gratifying to see your actions of wellness and self-care inspire your friends and family. I love to see my husband, Peter, enjoy learning a new skill, listen to an inspiring audiobook or the way to work, or connect with a friend. All of these are ways he de-stresses and takes care of himself.

## Self-Care Makes You More Generous

When we are anxious, unbalanced, and afraid, it can lead to a "lack mentality," "scarcity mindset," or the fear of limited love, resources, and opportunities. Those feelings of fear and needing safety and security can cause us to put ourselves first and others last. That might mean you can't listen to a family member's issue, you forget a friend's birthday, or you feel jealous at a colleague's success. When your own cup is full, you can freely give others more time, love, and energy.

## Self-Care Has a Ripple Effect

Each small action and interaction has an impact on someone else, for better or worse: the barista who makes your latte in the morning, your colleagues, your children, your parents, your friends. When you are feeling at peace and grateful, you can pass that energy along. Strive to leave the people you encounter in your day better than you found them. A smile, a compliment, or a bit of patience and compassion can go a long way. Sprinkle that sh*t like confetti!

# five-minute self-care practices

You don't have to carve out an entire evening of self-care for it to benefit you. Try adding these simple habits into your day when you need a bit of mindfulness amongst the mess.

## Morning Tea Practice

When you make your morning tea, be present in your mind and body while you slowly pour hot water over the tea. Let the tea steep, sip slowly, and feel the beneficial plant ingredients trickle through your body.

## Journaling Positive Affirmations & Gratitude

Make it a practice to take note of things you are grateful for, no matter how small. Take it a step further and write them out in the present tense. "I am grateful for a fun and inspiring workday." "I am grateful to be my healthiest self." Over time you might find the things you practice gratitude for expand, and the things you are striving for come to fruition. I keep a thorough gratitude list on my phone that I refer to when I need a pick-me-up. A wise person once said, "It's impossible to be grateful and anxious at the same time."

## Morning Tonic-Making

Practice trying out a new inspiring tonic (like one from this book!) to suit the mood you'd like to set for the day. Lately I've been sparking energy and inspiration with Green Mylk (page 61) or Coconut Beauty Water (page 56).

## Relationship Gratitude Tracking

Use a journal or your phone to track something you appreciate about your significant other or a family member or friend. Over time you might just notice your relationship bursting with mutual appreciation.

## One-Minute Meditation

Stress can make us hold our breath or take shallow breaths without realizing it, often leading to tension or headaches. While it's not always realistic to take five minutes out of the day to close your eyes and meditate, one minute of slow, deep breathing can still have benefits. Wherever you are, sit in stillness and inhale deeply through your nose. Let your belly fill with air, focusing as much on your breath as possible. Slowly breathe out through your mouth, paying attention to your belly retracting. Repeat three or four times.

## Subscribing to the Positive

Set an intention to consume inspirational and positive content that gives you a fresh perspective every day. Curate your social media, bookshelves, email lists, and YouTube to help you feel and become your best.

## Unsubscribing from the Junk

On the flip side, rid your inbox (and brain) of emails, social media accounts, and marketing that leave you feeling less-than or lacking.

## Reaching Out

Connect with that person you haven't checked in with for a while. Just a simple "thinking of you" can spark joy and make all the difference.

## Sh*t Talk

Use your journal to write out your negative thoughts, worries, frustrations, and anxiety. Don't be shy; let it all out. You'd be surprised how cathartic it can be!

## Visualization

Close your eyes and envision the best possible outcomes for yourself. Remove any judgment or question of "how?"—just let your mind wander there. I find visualization easiest to practice first thing in the morning before getting out of bed, or while enjoying my morning tonic.

# super fundamentals

Hopefully at this point you have slowed down, changed into your comfy pants, and are feeling a bit inspired to check in with yourself about your current self-care routine. Psst—there are plenty more juicy tips to come! Ready to get into the kitchen? We'll dig into some of the practical side of making tonics: the techniques, ingredients, and tools that will set you up for sweet superfood success. Let's get shaking, shall we?

# what's the deal with adaptogens?

Adaptogens are edible plants and mushrooms that can help your body adapt to daily stress—emotional, physical, or biological. While adaptogens have recently gained royalty status in the wellness world, these powerful plants have been used to treat ailments and boost performance for thousands of years. Adaptogens have the unique ability to assess what the body needs and to *adapt* to help maintain homeostasis. When we consume adaptogens, their organic properties and compounds work to help balance our systems. Ashwagandha, tulsi, chaga, maca, and goji berries are a few examples of adaptogens we'll get comfortable with in this book. If you struggle with frequent high stress, low energy, low immunity, low libido, low moods, or menstrual irregularities, adaptogens can be a beneficial part of your wellness practice.

I have found incorporating adaptogens into my routine has helped me function under high stress and enjoy quality sleep, while keeping my energy and mental clarity in check. (In other words: fewer anxiety-ridden days, better focus, and more zzz's.) In this book, you will see adaptogens used in recipes in a way that will make it fun and easy to incorporate them into your day—for example, incorporating energizing cordyceps mushroom into your coveted afternoon iced coffee (see Iced Power Mocha on page 66). Instead of swallowing back tinctures or capsules (and more often than not, forgetting to), I have found success adding powders into everything from smoothies to sauces to desserts. I especially love maca's nutty flavor in the delectable Salted Tahini "Caramel" (page 180).

To dig more into specific adaptogens and their benefits, head to page 26.

## Superfoods

Defined as a "nutrient-rich food considered to be especially beneficial for health and well-being," the term *superfood* is not regulated, and you'll find it splashed over everything from gummy bears to pizza crust in your grocery store. While it may take a more discerning eye to cut the marketing fluff from real, beneficial foods these days, I believe that superfoods are still worth celebrating for the amazing wellness-promoting and disease-preventing properties they possess.

In this book, superfoods are used to describe nutrient-dense whole foods found as close to their natural form as possible. Cacao, honey, coconut, chia, leafy greens, and miso are a few of my favorites that we'll celebrate for both their body benefits and the amazing flavor they bring to recipes. You'll notice the adaptogens we'll discuss also fall under the category of superfoods for their extensive nutritional profiles and unique ability to help the body maintain homeostasis.

A good practice for reaping the most benefits of superfoods is to buy and consume them in the least-processed format possible. For example, go for the fresh or frozen blueberries over the packaged berry trail mix. Supplementing with chaga in a homemade tonic will likely benefit you more than store-bought chocolate chaga almond butter (however yummy that sounds). Eat sweet potato crackers for their deliciousness, not as your antioxidant source for the day. We'll talk more about superfoods and their benefits on page 26.

## Following (or Not Following) the Recipes

I am a firm believer that a recipe should be a guideline, not a rule. The tonics in this book are especially free-flowing and conducive to tweaks based on your mood, the season, and your personal tastes. Feel free to color outside the lines, riff on the recipes, and use what you have in your pantry. Most importantly, making tonics should be a fun and enjoyable practice that you look forward to each day.

## Recipe Benefits

Included with the recipes in this book you will notice a benefit or benefits that correlate to each one, such as "Skin-Loving," "Energizing," or "Digestion-Supporting." These are meant to inspire you and inform you about the composition of the tonics, so you can consider ways to fit them into your day. Need a pick-me-up? Head toward a recipe marked "Mood-Boosting" or "Energizing." Looking for something to help prepare you for sleep? Keep an eye out for "Sleep-Promoting" or "Stress-Relieving."

## Using Adaptogens and Superfoods

This book celebrates superfoods and adaptogens that are at once wonderfully delicious and wholesomely beneficial. Depending on your current lifestyle, they also can be expensive, hard to find, and overwhelming to learn about all at once. I know what it is like to open a book and be discouraged by the long list of new-to-you ingredients. To combat this, I have designed the recipes in this book to be delicious with or without the recommended adaptogen powders or superfoods—you'll see that many ingredients are listed as optional. It's not necessary for you to go out and splurge on ten types of new ingredients—that is likely to overwhelm you (and your bank account). As you get more and more comfortable with making tonics, your repertoire and pantry will grow naturally. To get started, you can use what you have on hand, or invest in a few products that reflect your favorite flavors and the benefits you'd like to receive—for example, reishi powder for stress or cacao for energy and mood. To learn more about the superfoods used in this book, check out Superfoods 101 on page 26. Don't let the goal of perfection get in the way of trying something new!

## Tools

It has taken me a decade to stock my kitchen with a lot of the "right" tools for tonic recipes, and I wouldn't expect you to have everything on hand right away. Don't be afraid to use shortcuts, borrow a friend's tools, or take creative liberties to try out a new recipe. My first blender was an immersion blender borrowed from my mom, and it took many years of matcha lattes before I invested in my first twenty-dollar matcha whisk (forks did the job for a long time). See Your Tonics Toolbox on page 34 for more on specific tools for tonic-making.

## Tasting

Want to be a better cook? Here's something I learned in my job as a recipe developer: taste your work as you go. Before presenting a final dish to the Head of Culinary, I would taste and retaste, adjusting seasoning as necessary along the way, to make sure it was headed in the right direction. Making tonics is no different: the more you taste, the better you get at finding your perfect flavor balance. When following a recipe in this book, be sure to taste as you go, and make sure the final product is suited to your liking as well. It's your tonic, after all.

## Plant-Based Milks

When I am not whizzing up my own All-Purpose Plant Milk (page 45), I am staying stocked up with a variety of store-bought plant-based milks for tonics, cooking, and more. The store-bought milk that I most often use is oat milk because of its neutral flavor and luxurious creamy mouthfeel. It works beautifully for a variety of purposes: frothing in a latte, adding richness to oatmeal, or giving a smoothie a creamy component. Recipes that use plant-based milk will often specify the recommended milk or leave the option open if it doesn't impact the recipe. Most often, using your favorite milk or whatever you have on hand will suffice.

# Sweeteners

I'm a big fan of sweeteners that do double duty by creating a balanced flavor profile and bringing essential nutrients. Like plant-based milks, sweeteners will be recommended on a recipe basis, but you are welcome to use your preferred choice.

Liquid sweeteners like maple syrup are great because they dissolve quickly in cold tonics and provide a subtle level of sweetness. Coconut sugar is nutty and caramel-like and great in place of brown sugar for baking. Raw honey dissolves well in hot tonics and provides added benefits.

When adding sweeteners, it's best to start small and add more as you go. If your lifestyle omits the use of these sweeteners, the tonics also work with a dash of stevia or monk fruit, or you can remove the added sweetener entirely. In most recipes you will find a suggested level of sweetener to add, but feel free to trust your own taste buds and use more or less. Like seasoning with salt, it's always best to start with a small amount and add more sweetness to taste.

# Healthy Fats

Healthy fats are finally seeing their day in the sun, thanks to an upswing in high-fat diets and the widely available knowledge about their many benefits. Trendy or not, healthy fats in foods like avocado, hemp seeds, coconut, chia seeds, and almonds are vital to energy, nutrient absorption, immunity, and heart health.

Consuming healthy fats as a part of your diet has a positive impact on mental clarity, satiety, and well-being. Many recipes in this book include a smidge of coconut oil, ghee, or nut butter to boost the health benefits and flavor impact.

Fats take longer than carbohydrates to digest, which reduces the impact food has on your blood sugar levels and keeps you satiated between meals. My favorite benefit is the velvety mouthfeel fats bring, which makes the sipping experience that much more enjoyable. Look for healthy fats in Super Coffee (page 62), Wind-Me-Down Golden Mylk (page 168), and Adaptogenic Açai Smoothie Bowl (page 78).

# Salt

Many of these recipes call for a pinch of salt. Adding salt is a chef's trick to balance and emphasize the other flavors in the recipe. A scant amount of unrefined salt can make your watermelon smoothie burst with flavor, or add delicious contrast to your sweet granola. When salt is listed as a recipe ingredient in this book, it is referring to fine-grain sea salt or Himalayan pink salt (see Pink Salt, page 33). Look for salt to add that extra something to Salted Caramel Cashew Granola (page 82), Boosted Sea Salt Espresso Brownies (page 154), and Spicy Grapefruit Detox Margarita (page 143).

## Herbs & Spices

Herbs and spices deserve a place in your superfood pantry for the amazing health benefits, flavor, and complexity they can bring to a dish. I love to add an earthy bite of turmeric to refreshing drinks, as in Turmeric Chia Tonic (page 58), or the depth of cinnamon and ginger to hot drinks, like Sexy Superfood Hot Cacao (page 140).

For the sake of ease and accessibility, many of the recipes in this book call for dried herbs and spices. (I can't always find fresh turmeric at my grocery store, for example, but I always have dried handy.) But if you have the fresh ingredient on hand, that's wonderful. You can swap out dried herbs and spices for their fresh counterparts using the following ratio:
1 tablespoon minced fresh herbs/spices = 1 teaspoon dried herbs/spices.

### a note on the ingredients in this book

Dear friends, remember the content provided in this book is for informational purposes only and not meant to treat or diagnose any condition. You should always consult your healthcare provider, especially if you are pregnant or nursing, before trying a new herb, adaptogen, supplement, or superfood to make sure it is right for you. Many superfoods have contraindications (such as ashwagandha or goji berries), so if you are taking any prescription medications, it is especially important to get the go-ahead before you consume them. Never give a supplement to a child before checking with your pediatrician.

Superfoods and adaptogens are amazing plants that can benefit everything from your sex life to your mental health, but remember to treat them as a small piece of the puzzle that is your health and wellness. They are not a Band-Aid solution or cure-all but rather a part of a lifestyle that includes plenty of fresh whole foods, quality sleep, movement, passion, and love.

# superfoods 101

Meet the gang! Below you will find a list of vibrant, joy-giving superfoods, adaptogens, and plant ingredients that are featured in this book's recipes. These superfood pantry staples were curated for their ability to tick all the boxes: delicious to consume, packed with functional, health-promoting benefits, easy to work with, and relatively easy to source and purchase.

## Açai Berries

Açai berries are a wonderful skin food, as they are bursting with anti-oxidants and even contain high levels of essential fatty acids, amino acids, and dietary fiber. Pureed açai can be purchased in frozen packets, but for simplicity's and budget's sake, I love having the powdered product on hand. Both frozen açai and açai powder will work in my recipes.

## Activated Charcoal

Food-grade activated charcoal is a fine black powder made from coconut shells. While it now reigns as a trendy detox powder that flushes toxins and banishes bloating, charcoal has been used for centuries as an antidote for poison. The black powder has a unique ability to bind with toxic substances and remove them from the body before they are absorbed. Activated charcoal can impact the absorption of some medications, so be sure to enjoy it separately from medications and consult your healthcare practitioner before consuming.

## Apple Cider Vinegar

Full of probiotics and good-for-you nutrients, organic raw apple cider vinegar can aid in digestion by stimulating stomach acid and bolstering healthy gut bacteria. You can find apple cider vinegar in pure liquid form, as well as supplement tablets or gummies. Be warned: the pure vinegar is sour and powerful stuff! Enjoy up to 2 tablespoons per day, diluted with water.

## Ashwagandha

This is my favorite adaptogen and one of the most powerful plants on earth! Ashwagandha is a well-known stress-busting adaptogen, renowned for its ability to regulate hormone levels, relieve stress, and aid in sleep. Its flavor is earthy and bitter and pairs well with chocolate and coffee—or can even hide behind the other flavors in your smoothie.

## Bee Pollen

Bee pollen is vibrant golden granules harvested by bees, made up of flower blossoms, nectar, enzymes, honey, and bee secretions. Known as one of nature's most complete superfoods, bee pollen is high in protein, antioxidants, and energizing B-complex vitamins. The granules have a sweet, floral, and slightly bitter flavor, and I love to sprinkle them on smoothies and oatmeal or blend them into lattes for an added energy boost.

## Beet Powder

Made from dehydrated beets, beet powder brings a concentrated amount of nutrition and vibrant pink color to smoothies, oatmeal, baked goods, or granola. Studies show that consuming beets can boost blood flow, circulation, and energy, due to their high level of nitrates. I'm not wild about the taste of beets, but I find beet powder very palatable and especially delicious in a latte or smoothie.

## Butterfly Pea Flower

Butterfly pea flower comes from a vibrant blue flowering plant native to Asia. You'll often see it called "blue matcha," but it's not related to matcha or green tea at all. Its antioxidant properties, striking color, and mild flavor make it a popular coloring agent for baked goods, herbal teas, smoothies, and cocktails. You can find butterfly pea flower as whole dried flowers or a fine powder.

## Cacao

This raw, unprocessed version of chocolate is chock-full of benefits. Incredibly high in antioxidants and minerals, cacao has the ability to boost mood and increase feelings of well-being. Cacao naturally contains some caffeine, making it slightly stimulating. If you're sensitive to caffeine, enjoy raw cacao earlier in the day to avoid disrupting your sleep.

## CBD Oil

Found in the cannabis (marijuana) plant, CBD is a non-psychoactive compound (in other words, it won't get you buzzed). CBD oil is made by extracting CBD from the cannabis plant, then diluting it with a carrier oil like coconut or hemp seed. Its ability to ease symptoms of chronic pain and anxiety make it a go-to in my elixir kitchen. When adding CBD to recipes, follow the dosage instructions on the bottle and use a small amount to start. Try it out in the Chamomile Serenity CBD Latte (page 167) for a little pre-bedtime bliss.

## Chaga

Chaga mushrooms are powerful "immune-shrooms," coveted for their potent antioxidant and anti-inflammatory benefits. Earthy, rich, and slightly bitter, chaga can be found in tincture or pill form, or as a fine powder that can be stirred into coffee, hot chocolate, and tea.

# Chia Seeds

Loaded with fiber, healthy fats, and protein, chia seeds are a great way to sneak extra nutrients into smoothies, granola, and oatmeal. The insoluble fiber these small but mighty seeds contain helps keep you full longer while stimulating digestion and keeping you "regular." Cheers to chia!

# Chlorophyll

This trendy ingredient is the plant compound that gives your leafy green veggies their vibrant hue. Packed with powerful nutrients that help tame inflammation, it is linked to healthy skin and hair, gut health, and higher energy levels. The liquid version is widely available and even comes in flavors like peppermint and green apple (although you can buy it unflavored). Concentrations between brands can vary, so consult the packaging to confirm serving amounts.

# Cinnamon

This warming spice is blood-sugar-balancing and loaded with antioxidants and anti-inflammatory compounds. It acts as a natural sweetener, and its subtle warmth and dimension makes it a popular addition to many of the tonics and sweet eats in this book. Indulge in the benefits of cinnamon in the Chai Cinnamon Roll Baked Oatmeal (page 92) or Wind-Me-Down Golden Mylk (page 168).

# Coconut Oil

Coconut oil is rich in MCTs (medium-chain triglycerides), which digest easily and provide a quick source of fuel for the brain and body. There are two types of coconut oil to consider for your needs: refined and virgin. Refined coconut oil undergoes processing that removes the coconut aroma. It has a high smoke point and neutral flavor, which makes it a great option for cooking. Virgin (or unrefined) coconut oil has a subtly sweet coconut taste and aroma. It has a lower smoke point (350°F) but higher level of nutrients due to the minimal processing it undergoes. I prefer to use virgin coconut oil when making tonics (like Super Coffee on page 62) or recipes that don't involve cooking under high heat.

# Coconut Water

Also known as "nature's sports drink," coconut water refreshes and hydrates the body with a balance of electrolytes, making it the perfect post-workout tonic. Its high potassium level (more than four times that of bananas!) can help fight bloating by flushing out excess water from the body. Use it as a natural sweetener in your smoothie, drink it straight up, or try it in Coconut Beauty Water (page 56).

## Collagen

Collagen is a protein naturally produced in the body; it gives skin its elasticity and forms connective tissue to help seal and heal the lining of the gut. However, the natural production of collagen declines as we get older. Supplementing with collagen has been shown to have beauty benefits for skin, hair, nails, cellulite, and stretch marks. You can find it in a powder or liquid format, and it blends undetectably into teas, coffees, elixirs, oats, or smoothies.

## Cordyceps

Often considered the sexiest of all the fungi and known as "Himalayan Viagra," cordyceps is an adaptogen known for being stimulating to mood, energy, endurance, and libido. Cordyceps is a great mushroom for athletes, as it can help the body utilize oxygen more efficiently and enhance blood flow. It can be purchased in powder format as well as in a tincture or capsules. Its woodsy, nutty flavor makes it a great addition to your morning coffee, tea, latte, or smoothie.

## Ghee

An ancient Indian staple, ghee is butter that has been simmered slowly to remove all water, lactose, and casein, leaving only the purest form of the fat. Prized for its anti-inflammatory, digestive, and therapeutic properties, ghee is often considered suitable for those with lactose intolerance because it has only trace amounts of lactose. I love it for cooking because of its high smoke point (465°F compared to olive oil's, which is 400°F, and butter's, which is 350°F) and the decadent nutty flavor it lends to everything from Super Coffee (page 62) to roasted veggies and granola.

## Ginger Root

Zingy ginger has been used throughout the ages for its medicinal properties. It's a natural remedy for gastrointestinal distress, boosting digestion and soothing nausea. Ginger also relaxes and soothes the digestive tract, making it great if you're susceptible to uncomfortable bloating. Try adding fresh or dried ginger to curries, soups, stir-fries, and even smoothies for a zesty punch.

## Goji Berries

These chewy superberries have impressive benefits ranging from anti-aging to immune support. They are packed with antioxidants, like free-radical-busting vitamin C, and, for such a tiny fruit, contain a generous amount of fiber and protein. Goji are most often purchased as whole dried berries, but you can also find them in powder format. The superberries have a sweet, sour, and bitter flavor and

add fun texture and color to everything from sweet oatmeal to savory salads and bowls.

## Hemp Seeds

Hemp seeds are a delicious and convenient superfood, containing about 10 grams of protein in one 3-tablespoon serving and plenty of skin-loving and anti-inflammatory healthy fats. I like to think of these tiny seeds as nature's savory sprinkles. Keep them on hand to shower over salads and smoothie bowls or whizz into creamy dressings.

## Honey

In contrast to white refined sugar, raw honey is bursting with nutritional benefits like energizing B vitamins, enzymes, and immune-supporting properties. Look for raw, unpasteurized honey, which retains all the incredible benefits, and support your local beekeepers when possible. Honey is a delicious natural sweetener and adds a sweet and powerful punch to many of the hot tonics in this book. Try it in the Easy Chai Tea Concentrate (page 183).

## Lavender

Whether you're diffusing lavender essential oils at bedtime, sipping lavender tea, or lathering up with lavender body wash, this plant has been shown to boost mood and promote a sense of well-being. When shopping for lavender, keep in mind not all lavender varieties are edible, so look for English lavender (also called culinary lavender) that has a vibrant purple-blue color. Dried lavender is more potent than its fresh counterpart; keep in mind the ratio of 1 to 3 for dried lavender to fresh. A little lavender goes a long way; do not over-steep it, or it can turn bitter.

## Maca

Maca is a staple adaptogen in my pantry thanks to its nutty flavor and energizing, mood-boosting, and hormone-balancing benefits. A Peruvian root, it has been used traditionally in South America for more than two thousand years to help with energy, endurance, and libido. Its pleasing butterscotch-like flavor and powder form helps it blend seamlessly into oatmeal, baked goods, coffee, or smoothies.

## Maple Syrup

This dark, caramel-like liquid is my sweetener of choice for cold tonics and baked goods. I also reach for it any time I want to add a sweet, nutty flavor to a recipe. Pure maple syrup contains beneficial minerals and antioxidants but can spike your blood sugar if consumed in large quantities (a good thing to remind myself of when I'm drizzling maple syrup with abandon).

## Matcha

Green tea leaves that have been stone-ground into a delicate powder, matcha contains naturally occurring L-theanine, which gives it the unique ability to energize and calm the body at the same time. Matcha pairs deliciously with milk, fruit, and nutty flavors and can be enjoyed as a healthy coffee substitute. Ceremonial-grade matcha is widely regarded as the "Queen Bee" matcha by enthusiasts, but varying levels and price points of matcha are available on the market.

## Medjool Dates

Nature's chewy candy, dates are often used as a natural sweetener and provide fiber and antioxidants you won't find in refined sugar. Their plump and sticky flesh makes them a great base for desserts or energy balls. Try the magic of dates in the Chai Latte Bliss Balls (page 174). Like any sweetener, they are great to enjoy moderately and in balance with other whole foods.

## Miso

Salty, savory, and a bit funky, miso gets a prime spot in my fridge for its ability to pack a punch in soups, dressings, sauces, and marinades. Made with fermented soybeans, it's traditionally used in Japanese cooking and comes in sweet and dark varieties. For a lighter, sweeter flavor, I lean toward light miso (also called white miso). Find it in the refrigerated section near the fermented foods in Asian grocers or health-food stores.

## Nutritional Yeast

Used in savory plant-based cooking to add a slight cheesy flavor to foods, nutritional yeast is a great pantry companion and is packed with B vitamins and minerals. I love to blend it into salad dressings and soups for additional umami notes.

## Oats

Oats: a good-mood food! Oats are high in the dietary fiber beta-glucan, which helps nourish and restore healthy gut bacteria, improves digestion, and keeps you full and satisfied for longer. If that weren't enough to feel good about, oats are high in magnesium, a mineral that is linked to healthy sleep, improved mood, and mental health.

## Pink Salt

Unlike highly processed table salt, Himalayan pink salt contains more than eighty minerals and elements, including potassium, iron, and calcium. Pink salt helps stimulate digestion and detoxification, and keeps the body hydrated and energized thanks to the electrolytes it contains. I use pink salt daily in cooking, and often add a pinch to tonics or smoothies to emphasize other flavors.

## Reishi

Celebrated as "the Queen of Fungi," reishi mushrooms were once reserved only for royalty due to their rare and incredible health benefits. The powerful shrooms are loaded with antioxidants and are most commonly known to calm nerves and support healthy immune function. The earthy flavor of reishi pairs deliciously with the Chai Latte Bliss Balls (page 174).

## Spirulina

A hero in the plant-based community, spirulina is a source of vegan protein, antioxidants, and energy-boosting B vitamins. Widely available in tablets or powder form, spirulina can be blended into smoothies and juices, or stirred into water for an added boost of energy and detoxification support. You can find spirulina in both vibrant green and blue colors, but the blue variety is milder in flavor and brings the same benefits.

## Tulsi

An adaptogen known as "the Queen of Herbs," tulsi has been known in India and in Ayurvedic medicine for ages for its medicinal uses. Tulsi is extremely high in antioxidants and can help balance the production of stress hormones, lessening anxiety and depression. It has a slightly peppery and sweet flavor and can often be found in dried form or as part of a tea blend.

## Turmeric Root

An all-around super-healing herb, turmeric is best known for its ability to reduce inflammation and support the liver in detoxification. Used for centuries in India, turmeric brings its golden hue to some of my favorite tonics and culinary delights. Its earthy, bitter flavor is delicious in curries like Restorative Golden Dal (page 123), or balanced in a sweet application like oatmeal, baked goods, or smoothies.

# your tonics toolbox

I'm not one to rush out and buy the next insta-gadget until I know I will get lots of use out of the investment. Kitchen space is precious around here! For that reason, the tools I recommend in this section are pretty minimalistic. I do believe in keeping things in the home that spark joy (shout-out to Marie Kondo), and occasionally I will splurge on beautiful handmade ceramics or a high-speed blender that will last a decade. Tonic-making is a very personal ritual, something I encourage you to get comfortable with and make your own. Choosing the tools you work with is a part of that. Make it work with what you have on hand to start, but if you find yourself in the position to invest in a new tool, treasure it!

## Ceramic and Glass Mugs

Fill your cupboard with a few mugs that make you happy; they make the elixir experience that much more of a treat. I like to keep a few oversized tea mugs and artisan-crafted ceramics on hand, as well as clear glass mugs to show off a beautiful, colorful beverage like the Pink Warrior Latte (page 65).

## Tall Glasses

I always look forward to drinking my healthful tonics out of a beautiful glass. I have a few short ones for iced matcha lattes and some taller ones for iced teas and smoothies. Super-thin and clear glassware makes your colorful beverages pop.

## Reusable Straws

Who doesn't love slurping a cold beverage through a straw? For this reason, I stock a variety of reusable straws. Glass straws are beautiful, metal straws make your beverage magically taste more refreshing, and bamboo straws are lightweight for traveling.

## High-Speed Blender

For whizzing up ultra-creamy smoothies or quick blender lattes, I invested in a Blendtec eight years ago, and we are still attached at the hip. I have also worked with a Vitamix blender with amazing results. The warranties these machines offer can make them a worthwhile purchase if you plan to blend often. While a high-speed blender delivers optimal results for the recipes in this book, any blender you have on hand will work just fine.

## Bamboo Matcha Whisk

Great for preparing matcha or dissolving fine powders for hot chocolate or turmeric lattes, I love this tool because it creates a beautiful matcha foam, but you can absolutely use a fork or kitchen whisk instead.

## Glass Jars with Lids

Use these for cold-brewing teas in the fridge or for storing tonics or mylks. Repurposed jam, pickle, or nut butter jars work wonderfully.

## Small Saucepans

These are perfect for whisking up hot tonics. I use the same small-to-medium pot I use for cooking grains. Use any saucepan you have.

## Strainer

Sieve, sifter, strainer—just make sure it has fine mesh to capture all of the plant matter bits. I have a small one for straining single cups of tea and a larger one for straining big batches of iced tea.

## Tea Infuser

This is a key ingredient in making the perfect loose-leaf tea. Depending on the day, I'll use a reusable metal tea strainer or disposable tea sachet that I fill up with herbs. The latter is generally compostable and great for making tea lattes, because you can easily keep it in your mug as you sip.

## Citrus Squeezer

I only recently purchased a handheld citrus squeezer, and I can't believe how much precious lemon juice I've been missing out on all this time! Do yourself a favor and make your tangy tonics, salad dressings, and life a little easier by purchasing one of these gadgets. It removes the seeds for you and gets every last drop of delicious juice.

## Nut Milk Bag

I delayed getting one of these nifty cloth bags for ages because a mesh strainer/sieve works (almost) as well for straining homemade nut milk. The cloth material of the bag ensures a super-smooth, finely filtered homemade milk. It costs less than ten dollars and takes up very little room in your "everything" drawer.

# elevated everyday essentials

My motto? Romanticize the mundane, elevate the everyday, and do what you can to make the little moments feel special. These tonic "basics" are designed to be whipped up again and again, making your day a little more delicious. We'll talk tea, of course, and I'll spill my secrets for the perfect iced brew (page 40) and how to hydrate for dewy skin and energy (page 38), and I'll share my tricks for fuss-free homemade nut milks (page 45).

# how to drink more water

One of the first things I learned when studying holistic nutrition is that most of us are chronically dehydrated. Want more energy? Drink more water. Looking to improve your digestion? Drink more water! Since then it has stuck with me to make hydration an important part of my wellness routine. At any point in the day, you will find me with a bottle of plain water, coconut water or fruit-infused water, a cup of tea, or a prepared tonic (like one in the pages of this book!). Now, you ask, how do you boost your water intake when you aren't fond of the taste?

## Make it fun and easy

Invest in beautiful glassware and water bottles that you enjoy drinking out of. I have an oversized water bottle with a tight-fitting lid and straw that is always by my side—in the car, at work, and on my bedside table. Having a convenient and fun way to hydrate (especially on busy days) makes it much more likely you'll hydrate adequately. Your glowy skin will thank you!

## Make it flavorful

I used to work at a resort spa where every morning we'd fill a carafe with cold water and a rainbow of fresh fruit to create fruit-infused water. The spa guests happily slurped it down—I've never seen water so popular! Besides the array of delicious hydration recipes in this book, there are ways to instantly boost your water by infusing it with fresh herbs and fruits. There is no recipe or fancy tools required, just combine cold water with whatever inspires you. For extra flavor, try muddling the fruit or herbs with a spoon to release some of the flavors, or you can let the water infuse overnight. A few of my favorite infused-water combinations are: strawberry and cucumber slices; fresh mint leaves and lemon slices; orange and grapefruit slices; and raspberries and fresh basil leaves.

# two methods for incredible iced tea

Luckily for this tea biz owner, when summertime hits, tea lovers are still looking to get their fix of herbals. That's where the magical world of iced teas and tisanes comes in.

Once you get the hang of it, iced tea is a lot more fun than your average mug of hot tea, because the options to create different flavor combinations are endless. A simple tea bag, when combined with a few mix-ins, can transform a beverage into a refreshing and fruity hydrator (not to mention the star of your picnic lunch). If you're not an experienced tea nerd, creating a barista-worthy iced tea can be intimidating at first. (If you've ever created a bland, watery, or overly milky iced tea, you know what I mean!) To save you time and tea, I've spent many warm days playing scientist with iced tea and found what I believe to be the most foolproof methods for the perfect glass.

## the perfect glass of iced tea

This recipe is particularly great if you're in a hurry and just want one glass of iced tea for yourself. There are no fancy gadgets or complicated steps involved—just strongly brewed tea and plenty of ice!

**makes 1 glass**

2 tea bags or 1 tablespoon loose-leaf tea (any kind)

1 cup boiling water

Sweetener of your choice (optional)

To your favorite tall heatproof glass, add the tea bags and pour the boiling water over it. Cover and steep for 10 minutes (or as long as you can stand to wait). Remove the tea bags (strain the leaves if using loose tea). Sweeten to taste if desired. Top with a heaping cup of ice to cool instantly.

Stir in any fruit, herb, or milk additions (see page 42 for inspiration). Sip and be refreshed!

# cold brew tea

In the peak of summer, nothing feels more luxurious than having a pitcher of icy-cold herbal tea at the ready. It's beautiful, hydrating, and a delicious way to get a dose of high-vibe herbs and adaptogens into your day. My favorite way to accomplish this is with the cold brew tea method, which is just a fancy way of saying "steep the tea leaves in cold water." The good news is, cold brewing is especially forgiving, and it's difficult to over-steep or turn the tea leaves bitter. You'll just need to exercise a bit of patience to let the tea steep to its most flavorful potential.

In a glass jar or pitcher, combine the water and tea. Refrigerate for at least 8 hours and up to 3 days. The longer the tea steeps, the more concentrated the tea flavor will be.

Remove the tea bags (strain the leaves if using loose tea), stir in any desired additions, and serve cold. Enjoy!

**makes 1 quart (about 1 liter)**

1 quart (about 1 liter) cold water

3 tea bags or 2 tablespoons loose-leaf tea (any kind)

Fresh herb sprigs, citrus rounds or peels, berries, honey, or maple syrup for serving (optional)

# delicious iced tea combinations

Channel the mixologist in you to elevate your cup of tea with delicious mix-ins—no cup need ever be the same! Depending on the weather or your mood, play around with some of these proposed tea combinations. I've divided them into two categories: "Rich & Milky" provides a richer, latte-like cup of tea, while "Fresh & Fruity" works well when you want something refreshing and hydrating. For each category, I include the type of tea I'd recommend, but as always, you can experiment to see what you like best. When adding mix-ins to a glass of tea, start small with a splash of milk, teaspoon of sweetener, tablespoon of fruit, or dash of spices. Taste and adjust as desired.

## Rich & Milky

Earl Grey Tea + Lavender + Coconut Milk + Vanilla

Black Tea + Oat Milk + Cinnamon + Nutmeg + Ginger

Chai Tea + Coconut Milk + Cinnamon + Honey

Rooibos Tea + Lavender + Almond Milk + Cinnamon

Lavender Tea + Coconut Milk + Vanilla

Turmeric Tea + Almond Milk + Cinnamon

Matcha Tea + Mango + Almond Milk

Chamomile Tea + Coconut Milk + Honey

## Fresh & Fruity

Black Tea + Lemon + Fresh Mint

Black Tea + Peaches + Maple Syrup

Rooibos Tea + Strawberry + Vanilla

Peppermint Tea + Lemon + Honey

Hibiscus Tea + Pomegranate + Maple Syrup + Lime

Green Tea + Lemon + Raspberries + Fresh Mint

Green Tea + Peaches + Cucumber

Black Tea + Lemonade + Thyme

Earl Grey Tea + Peaches + Lemon

Ginger Tea + Lemon + Mint

Matcha Tea + Lime + Maple Syrup

# five easy-breezy plant-based milks

While I am the first to appreciate the convenience of store-bought plant milks, I also love the luxury of freshly whizzed coconuts with a hint of maple and vanilla bean. I've compiled some of my most successful, delicious, and versatile plant-based milks that are worth firing up the blender for. Whether you use a fancy nut milk bag or a strainer, a high-speed blender or a hand-me-down, there is rich satisfaction in blending your own plant-based milk to taste.

## all-purpose plant milk

Meet your new favorite everyday fifteen-minute plant-based milk! It's creamy enough for coffee but light enough for smoothies and drinking by the glass. Don't fret about soaking your cashews overnight. (Who has time for that?) This version uses a quick-soak method with just-as-creamy results. The combination of coconut, hemp seeds, and cashews makes for a versatile, delicious, and nutrient-dense milk. The vanilla and sweetener make it super-sippable but can be omitted if you're using the milk for savory applications.

In a large bowl, combine the coconut flakes, hemp seeds, and cashews. Cover with boiling water and set aside to soak for 15 minutes.

Drain the nut mixture, discarding the soaking liquid. In a high-speed blender, combine the nut mixture and the remaining ingredients and blend for 2 minutes, until completely creamy and frothy. Strain through a nut milk bag or fine-mesh sieve into a large lidded jar or airtight container. The milk will keep fresh and delicious for up to 5 days in the fridge.

### makes about 3 cups

1 cup unsweetened coconut flakes

½ cup hemp seeds (see page 31)

½ cup raw cashews

Boiling water, for soaking

3½ cups warm water

1 teaspoon vanilla extract (optional)

1 to 3 tablespoons sweetener of your choice (optional)

Pinch of salt

Antioxidant-Rich • Skin-Loving • Rich in Healthy Fats • Anti-Inflammatory

# vanilla cashew creamer

If there's a plant milk recipe to inspire you to make your own, it should be this one. Without soaking or straining the cashews, you can whip this up in less time than it takes to find your favorite carton in the dairy-alternative aisle. It's lightly sweetened with honey and vanilla and will make you feel like Gwyneth P. as it luxuriously cascades into your coffee or tea. Just four ingredients (cashews, honey, vanilla, salt). No fillers, stabilizers, or thickeners in sight!

**makes about 2 cups**

½ cup raw cashews

1¾ cups warm water

1 to 2 tablespoons raw honey (see page 31)

1 teaspoon vanilla extract

Pinch of salt

In a high-speed blender, combine all the ingredients and blend for 60 to 90 seconds, until completely creamy and frothy. Transfer to a lidded jar or airtight container. This creamer will keep fresh and delicious for up to 5 days in the fridge.

---

**customize it**

This cashew creamer was designed to be extra creamy and add luxurious flavor and texture to your drinks. You can customize it by adding or reducing water to taste. Add ¼ cup more water to the recipe for a cashew "milk" and use less water for a creamer that's even more like, well, cream!

# cinnamon toast hemp milk

It doesn't get much more hipster than homemade hemp milk, does it? Skip the soaking and straining and throw hemp seeds and hot water straight into your blender to create a mean milk you'll want to use for smoothies, granola, and your morning chai latte. The touch of coconut oil is optional but adds frothiness and heft.

In a high-speed blender, combine all the ingredients and blend for 60 to 75 seconds, until creamy and frothy. Transfer to a lidded jar or airtight container. Hemp milk will keep fresh and delicious for up to 5 days in the fridge.

*Pictured on page 44*

**makes about 2 cups**

⅓ cup hemp seeds
(see page 31)

2 cups hot water

1 teaspoon coconut oil
(optional)

1 teaspoon vanilla extract

¾ teaspoon ground
cinnamon

2 teaspoons maca powder
(optional)

1 to 3 tablespoons maple
syrup or other sweetener

Pinch of salt

# strawberry dream milk

I wasn't one of those lucky kids who chugged vibrant pink milk straight from the carton, but this wholesome strawberry oat milk version makes my '90s dreams come true. Revel in the luxurious strawberry satisfaction straight up, on ice, with granola, or in the Strawberry Matcha Latte (page 112).

### makes about 2 cups

2 cups All-Purpose Plant Milk (page 45), or your favorite plant-based milk

¾ cup strawberries

1 tablespoon raw honey (see page 31)

1 teaspoon vanilla extract

Pinch of beet powder for added color (optional)

In a high-speed blender, combine all the ingredients and blend for 30 to 45 seconds, until smooth. Strain through a fine-mesh sieve or nut milk bag to remove any seeds, or enjoy as is. Transfer to a lidded jar or airtight container and store in the fridge for up to 3 days.

# toasted coconut milk

Yes, you read that right—*toasted* coconut. The nutty flavor from toasted coconut brings so much more depth of flavor than your standard coconut milk. Creamy, nutty, and delicious, this milk works wonderfully in an elevated tea latte like the Toasted Coconut London Fog (page 70), in coffee, or with granola or oatmeal.

### makes about 4 cups

2 cups unsweetened coconut flakes

4 cups warm water

1 tablespoon vanilla extract

Pinch of salt

2 to 3 teaspoons maple syrup or raw honey, plus more as needed

To a large skillet, add the coconut flakes. Toast over medium heat for 3 to 5 minutes, stirring occasionally, until golden. Transfer to a small bowl to cool slightly.

In a high-speed blender, combine the coconut and the remaining ingredients. Blend for 60 seconds, until smooth and frothy. Strain through a fine-mesh sieve or nut milk bag. Taste and add more sweetener if desired. Transfer to a large lidded jar or airtight container and store in the fridge for up to 3 days.

# five tips for killer smoothies

### 1. Boost Them with Superfoods and Adaptogens

If you find you forget to use up those superfoods lurking in the back of your pantry (guilty!), your daily smoothie can be an effortless way to get them into your diet.

Superfood boosters like collagen, goji berries, chia, chaga, flax, hemp seeds, oats, and protein powder can add substance, satiety, and benefits to your morning sip. Hemp seeds are included in the Adaptogenic Açai Smoothie Bowl (page 78).

### 2. Disguise Veggies

I personally don't jump out of bed excited for the taste of leafy greens in the morning. That's why I have developed a roster of smoothies that do a fabulous job of hiding a couple servings of veggies. Frozen cauliflower adds creaminess and heft to the Cacao-Hazelnut Smoothie (page 77). Frozen baby spinach, kale, and zucchini are also great choices for bulking up your smoothie with veg without compromising flavor.

### 3. Add Protein, Fat, and Fiber for Fullness

If you've ever scoffed at smoothies being a hearty breakfast, I'll be the one to tell you that you might not have loaded them up with enough protein, fat, and fiber.

For a hit of protein, sprinkle in plant-based protein powder or bump it up with hemp seeds, pumpkin seeds, tofu, or Greek yogurt.

To add healthy fats, consider avocado, hemp seeds, almond butter, or coconut oil.

To fiber up, blend in chia seeds, flaxseeds, leafy greens, berries, nuts, or oats, like in the Oatmeal Cookie Smoothie (page 173).

### 4. Add Flavor Bombs

A trick to keep your daily smoothie exciting is whizzing in unexpected herbs, spices, and flavor-packed ingredients. Adding fresh basil, mint, citrus zest, a pinch of salt, nut butters, or a splash of fresh juice is how the smoothie pros make their elixirs taste so dang good. Try out the zing of fresh ginger and lime in the Tropical Beach Babe Smoothie (page 74).

## 5. Keep It Icy

Smoothies are so much more sippable when they're cold. Keep it chilly by cutting all your fruits and veggies into small chunks and then freezing them. The added benefit is your groceries have a much longer life. Spotted brown bananas, half-eaten avocados, and wilted fresh herbs, and greens all get piled into my freezer, reducing food waste and my grocery bill.

## frothing 101: how to froth milk like it's hot

**Handheld Milk Frother**—This gadget froths like a dream but can get messy (IYKYK). Heat the milk and transfer to a tall glass or jar with high sides. Froth for 10 to 20 seconds, until you reach your desired consistency.

**French Press**—I've never been cool enough to own a French press, but I've seen wonderful results when it's used to froth hot (or even cold) milk. Just pour the milk into the press and pump the plunger up and down for 10 to 15 seconds, until foamy.

**Mason Jar**—This method feels a bit rudimentary, but hey, it does the job! Simply heat the milk and add it to a sealed mason jar (or other jar with a lid). Make sure the lid is fully sealed (learned this lesson way too many times!) and shake vigorously for 30 to 60 seconds, until frothy.

**Electric Milk Frother**—I splurged on one of these tabletop numbers by Breville for Lake & Oak's headquarters. Great for the tea latte lover, bulletproof coffee drinker, or hot cocoa queen. Just add all the ingredients to the frother and it will steam *and* froth your milk for you—heavenly!

**Blender**—Popular for its ease and "mix-ability," this method is reserved for when I want to thoroughly dissolve fats like coconut oil or nut butter into my tonic (see Easy Blender Matcha Latte, page 69). Simply heat the milk or tonic and add to the blender. Blend for 30 to 60 seconds, until frothy and wonderful.

**Steam Wand**—The most luxurious and expensive option is the professional espresso machine with a steam wand. It creates a beautiful micro-foam that will take your tonic or latte to barista-worthy heights.

**Practice being present.** You can practice being in the present at any time during the day. Simply focus on what you're doing right now, not on the past or the future.

**Free up time.** Simplifying your life in general is a way to free up time to do the stuff you want to do. Unfortunately, it can be hard to find time to even think about how to simplify your life. If that's the case, free up just a few short minutes a day for thinking about how, [...] extensively, free up [...]

# get up & glow

Morning is my favorite time to practice making super tonics. Your taste buds are fresh, your body is thirsty, and there's promise of a great day ahead. Morning tonics are all about boosting hydration, bolstering energy, promoting digestion, and celebrating a new day. If you're feeling under the weather or uninspired, a healing elixir is a comforting tool to have handy.

# design your dream morning

Social media and the personal development world can make it seem like everyone who has it together is rocking a stellar morning routine. As though if you're not waking up with the scent of lavender wafting from your bedside table and an educational podcast playing, you're doing it wrong. Are you thinking the 5:00 a.m. meditations, mantras, or workouts are not your thing? I get you—I'm an unruly Aquarius who prefers to buck any concepts of schedules and routine. But when I was going through a particularly stressful time in life, I finally caved and put some love and care into creating space for a morning ritual. And guess what? It really helped.

If you're someone who dreads mornings or wakes up feeling a bit melancholy, a mindful start can be especially beneficial for your day. A solid morning routine will light you up, get your creative juices going, and set the right intentions for the day. How about an 8:00 a.m. dance party? Latte and chill in bed? Moisturize from head to toe? The morning is your oyster.

My ritual evolves based on my schedule and the season, but I try to write in my gratitude journal every morning, drink a hydrating tonic, and spend some time in nature. The rest is a bonus.

We all have morning duties that are less-than-glamorous (such as making lunches for three humans in record time or taking out the recycling at the crack of dawn), but carving out some me time can have a ripple effect on your mental wellness and life.

To get your creative juices flowing, I've included a few ideas for constructing a killer morning ritual. Check off the ones that look like they would bring you joy and get you planning your best morning ever.

- [ ] Express gratitude to your loved ones

- [ ] Check in with your goals

- [ ] Tidy or declutter your space

- [ ] Take in a TED Talk

- [ ] Scribble new ideas

- [ ] Journal your thoughts

- [ ] Make a hot tea or coffee

- [ ] Read some good news

- [ ] Take a photo journal

- [ ] Have a hot-and-cold shower (it boosts circulation and energy!)

- [ ] Get inspired by a new healthy recipe (Pinterest is my favorite source for this)

- [ ] Visualize an awesome day ahead (especially if you're feeling meh)

- [ ] Go phone-free before 9:00 a.m.

- [ ] Do something nice for someone

- [ ] Take your supplements (set an alarm to remind you)

- [ ] Make a hydrating tonic

- [ ] Spend time in nature

- [ ] Sit in stillness (even five minutes can make a difference)

- [ ] Moisturize and massage your body

- [ ] Plan your day

- [ ] Light a candle

- [ ] Prioritize your to-do list

- [ ] Move your body (whatever that looks like for you)

- [ ] Look at your dream board

- [ ] Listen to high-vibe music

- [ ] Check in on a friend

- [ ] Meal-plan for the day ahead

- [ ] Read something inspiring

- [ ] Listen to a mood-boosting podcast

- [ ] Dance

- [ ] Enjoy a luxurious skin-care routine

This popular combination of apple cider vinegar, lemon, and cayenne is often touted as a drinkable "reset button" for your insides. While this tonic is probably not going to erase last night's mistakes, raw apple cider vinegar contains gut-friendly properties, and the lemon juice is packed with skin-brightening vitamin C. This drink is tangy and refreshing, and it pairs well with sunshine and good vibes.

# apple cider vinegar lemon-aid

### makes 1 tonic

1½ cups water

2 tablespoons fresh lemon juice

1 teaspoon organic raw apple cider vinegar

1 teaspoon maple syrup

Pinch of cayenne pepper (optional)

In a tall glass, combine all the ingredients. Stir well to combine. Sip and pucker up!

First thing in the morning, our bodies are extra dehydrated after a night's rest, so it's a good idea to hydrate and jump-start cleansing. This beauty water with vibrant green liquid chlorophyll is also effective as a pick-me-up throughout the day or a post-workout beverage.

# coconut beauty water

### makes 1 drink

½ cup water

1 cup coconut water (see page 28)

1 teaspoon liquid chlorophyll (see page 28)

In your favorite glass, combine all the ingredients and stir. Top with ice if desired. Sip and soak up the green beauty.

*Pictured on page 12*

This golden tonic may sound (and taste) glamorous, but it's actually just a boosted-up, naturally sweetened lemonade (and a great way to get your daily dose of turmeric). You can make this elixir with or without the chia, but I love the added digestive help these mighty seeds offer. The only hard part is waiting for them to plump up into their delicious jelly-like orbs. Shake this tonic up before bed, pop it in the fridge, and start your next day on a sunny note.

# turmeric chia tonic

**makes 1 tonic**

2 cups water

Juice of 1 lemon

½ teaspoon ground turmeric or 1 teaspoon freshly grated turmeric

2 teaspoons maple syrup (optional)

2 teaspoons chia seeds (see page 28)

In a large shaker or lidded jar, combine all the ingredients and shake well. Refrigerate for at least 30 minutes or overnight, until the chia seeds are plumped. Shake again, pour into a tall glass, and enjoy slurping up the refreshing golden goodness.

Green juice meets almond milk . . . stay with me! This vibrant green tonic drinks like an icy-cold glass of vanilla almond milk—you'll barely notice you're consuming any greens! I blended it up one day when I wanted to give my body a jolt of leafy greens in a hurry—without the rest of the typical smoothie ingredients. It's refreshing, energizing, and a great complement to your breakfast; or try it as an afternoon pick-me-up.

# green mylk

In a high-speed blender, combine all the ingredients. Blend for 30 to 60 seconds, until completely smooth. Serve over more ice. Sip and enjoy!

**makes 1 beverage**

1 cup almond milk or oat milk

1 cup baby spinach

½ cup ice cubes, plus more for serving

½ teaspoon vanilla extract

½ teaspoon spirulina powder (optional)

This moderately caffeinated pre-workout tonic combines matcha powder, for sustained, feel-good energy, with spirulina, the blue-green algae superfood packed with energizing B vitamins and protein. Coconut water is a delicious and ultra-hydrating base for this beverage, but if you don't have coconut water on hand, plain water works just fine. If you're not working out, this elixir is also a great solution to the dreaded 3:00 p.m. energy slump.

# clean green energy tonic

In a glass, combine the matcha and spirulina and a dash of the coconut water. Whisk until dissolved and tiny bubbles form. Top with ice and the remaining coconut water. Sip and revive.

**makes 1 tonic**

½ teaspoon matcha powder

¼ teaspoon spirulina powder

1 cup coconut water

Since I'm an advocate for all things herbal, it can surprise people to hear that espresso runs through my veins. If you're with me on this, why not take advantage of your daily caffeine habit and toss in some functional mix-ins that go the extra mile (or quite literally help you run an extra mile)? The combination of coconut oil, collagen, and warming spices makes for a powered-up brew that will keep you satiated and energized longer than your traditional cup of joe. You can use either a blender or a milk frother to prepare this bubbly brew.

# super coffee

### makes 1 drink

1 cup brewed coffee

1 teaspoon coconut oil, ghee, or coconut butter

1 tablespoon collagen powder (see page 29)

½ teaspoon ashwagandha powder

1 teaspoon raw honey (optional)

Bee pollen, CBD oil, ground cinnamon, ground turmeric, nutmeg, or ground ginger, for mix-ins (choose 1 or a combo; optional)

In a high-speed blender, combine all the ingredients. Blend for 15 to 30 seconds, until creamy and frothy. Pour into a mug and enjoy right away.

As a tea purveyor, I've learned that many of us are trying to break up with—or at least have a more casual relationship with—caffeine. How to perk up without coffee, you ask? That's where energizing adaptogens and plants enter the chat. In this beauty bev, energy-boosting beets mingle with the endurance-enhancing cordyceps mushroom. In the hotter months, I love making this into a "pink milk" in a tall glass with lots of ice. What does it taste like? Think adult strawberry milk, with a hint of beet's earthiness and warming spices.

# pink warrior latte

In your favorite mug, combine the beet powder, cinnamon, ginger, maple syrup, vanilla, collagen, and cordyceps. Add a splash of water and whisk to make a paste.

Froth or heat the milk and pour it over the beet mixture. Stir gently to combine. Sprinkle an extra pinch of cinnamon over top.

### makes 1 latte

¾ teaspoon beet powder (see page 27)

Pinch of ground cinnamon, plus more for garnish

Pinch of ground ginger

1 to 2 teaspoons maple syrup or honey

¼ teaspoon vanilla extract

1 teaspoon collagen powder

½ teaspoon cordyceps powder

1 cup plant-based milk

### ice it, baby

Alternatively, skip heating the milk and serve the latte over ice.

Picture this: chocolate milk meets iced coffee on an upscale vacation in Tulum. Energizing raw cacao and cordyceps pair deliciously to create this elixir that is one part dessert, one part coffee, and 100 percent delicious rocket fuel. Just stir, sip, and conquer.

Energizing • Mood-Boosting • Mind-Clarifying • Libido-Boosting

# iced power mocha

## makes 1 drink

1½ teaspoons raw cacao powder (see page 27)

1 to 2 teaspoons maple syrup

¼ teaspoon cordyceps powder

1 cup brewed coffee

Handful of ice

Milk or cream, for serving (optional)

In a tall glass, combine the cacao powder, maple syrup, and cordyceps. Add a splash of water and whisk to make a paste. Pour the coffee over and top with ice.

If desired, add a splash of milk or cream (this creates a beautiful ripple effect I'm very fond of). Stir, admire your creation, and bliss out.

### switch it up
Swap the cacao powder out for 1 tablespoon chocolate protein powder for a satisfying protein-packed tonic.

The magic of this matcha latte is thanks to the blender, which transforms nut butter and water into a frothy nut milk in seconds. Combined with the matcha and raw honey, it makes a barista-worthy latte with less effort than your morning skin routine. For an even creamier, foamier latte, increase the nut butter or add a smidge of coconut oil.

# easy blender matcha latte

In a high-speed blender, combine all the ingredients. Blend for 30 to 45 seconds, until frothy and combined. Taste and add more honey if desired. Enjoy right away.

### switch it up
Swap out the hot water for room-temperature water and serve over ice.

### makes 1 latte

1 teaspoon matcha powder

1 cup almost-boiling water

2 teaspoons nut butter (cashew, almond, or hazelnut work well)

1 teaspoon raw honey or other sweetener, plus more as needed

¼ teaspoon vanilla extract (optional)

## brewing the perfect matcha

Hot water bolsters the delicate vegetal taste of matcha, but boiling water will turn it bitter. If your kettle has a thermometer, boil the water to 175°F (80°C). If not, bring the water to a boil and let it rest for 3 to 5 minutes before using.

Like a warm hug on a chilly day, a traditional London Fog is a tea latte made up of strongly brewed Earl Grey tea, vanilla sugar syrup, and frothed whole milk. This wholesome version is naturally sweetened and uses homemade toasted coconut milk to round out the bold black tea. If you're not using toasted coconut milk, just swap in any plant-based milk and add a few drops of vanilla extract to the brewed tea.

# toasted coconut london fog

**makes 1 latte**

2 tea bags or 1 tablespoon loose-leaf Earl Grey tea

¾ cup boiling water

1 to 2 teaspoons maple syrup or coconut sugar

¾ cup Toasted Coconut Milk (page 48) or any plant-based milk

Rose petals, toasted coconut flakes, and/or ground cinnamon, for garnish (optional)

To your favorite oversized mug, add the tea bags and pour the boiling water over it. Let steep, covered, for 5 minutes. Remove the tea bags (or keep them in for bolder flavor; strain the tea if using loose). Stir in the maple syrup.

Froth or heat up the milk and pour it over the steeped tea mixture. Garnish with any or all of the suggested toppings. Sip in cozy bliss.

## tea latte 101

For the most pronounced flavor in a tea latte, cover the tea as it's steeping and keep the tea bag in for *at least* 5 minutes. I like to keep the tea bag in even after I top it with milk for bolder flavor, but feel free to discard it at this point.

### switch it up

No espresso machine? Swap the espresso shot for ¾ cup strongly brewed coffee.

Not a fan of coffee? Nix the espresso and enjoy the spiced frothed milk on its own.

No cans of pumpkin puree were harmed in the making of this easy-as-pie pumpkin spice latte recipe. This streamlined PSL uses warming autumnal spices and maple syrup to bring the signature spicy-sweet sip. Ginger, nutmeg, cinnamon, and allspice make up most pumpkin pie spice blends, which also happen to be packed with anti-inflammatory benefits. Let's get cozy!

# nourishing pumpkin spice latte

Pour the espresso shot into your coziest mug.

In a small saucepan, warm the milk, maple syrup, pumpkin pie spice, vanilla, and ashwagandha (if using) over medium heat, whisking occasionally, until hot. Froth the milk mixture in the pan using a handheld milk frother (or see Frothing 101 on page 51 for more frothing methods).

Pour the frothed spiced milk over the espresso. Top with a pinch of cinnamon. Sip and soak up the cozy, spicy feels.

**makes 1 latte**

1 shot espresso

¾ cup oat or cashew milk

1 to 2 teaspoons maple syrup

½ teaspoon pumpkin pie spice (store-bought or see recipe below)

½ teaspoon vanilla extract

½ teaspoon ashwagandha powder (optional)

Pinch of ground cinnamon, for garnish

## make your own pumpkin pie spice blend

In a small bowl, combine 1 tablespoon ground cinnamon, ¾ teaspoon ground ginger, ¾ teaspoon nutmeg, and ¾ teaspoon ground cloves or allspice. Store in an airtight container at room temperature for up to 2 years.

I developed this smoothie with high hopes of transporting you to sunnier days beachside in Hawaii—think sun-kissed skin, salty air, and sand between your toes. This tropical smoothie channels that feeling with every sip. The vibrant hue comes from the blue-green algae spirulina, which sneaks in extra energy-giving antioxidants. No algae on hand? No worries, it's just as awesome without.

# tropical beach babe smoothie

### makes 1 bountiful smoothie

1½ cups water or coconut water (see page 28)

½ cup frozen mango pieces

¼ cup frozen pineapple pieces

½ cup frozen banana pieces

1 heaping cup baby spinach or baby kale

2 teaspoons hemp seeds

¼-inch piece fresh ginger (skin-on is fine)

Juice of ½ lime

1 teaspoon green or blue spirulina powder (optional)

To a high-speed blender, add the water, followed by the remaining ingredients. Blend for 60 seconds, or until smooth and creamy. Sip and soak up the tropical vibes.

My partner, Peter, is a Nutella-by-the-spoonful kind of guy. He's known for scouting out great prices on oversized jars of the beloved chocolate-hazelnut spread. I used to judge his nutty habit, but I've come to appreciate a spoonful of the good stuff while curled up on the couch. This rich-yet-refreshing smoothie packs pure chocolatey satisfaction in every sip. Sometimes, if my to-do list looks particularly daunting, I'll add a shot of espresso to kick it up a notch. Chocolate protein powder can be swapped out for extra cacao powder in a pinch.

# cacao-hazelnut smoothie

In a high-speed blender, combine all the ingredients. Blend for 40 to 60 seconds, until smooth and creamy. Sip and bliss out.

**makes 1 smoothie**

1 cup plant-based milk

1 tablespoon raw cacao powder (see page 27)

1 tablespoon hazelnut butter

1 tablespoon chocolate protein powder

1 cup frozen banana pieces

¾ cup frozen cauliflower pieces

¾ teaspoon chaga powder (optional)

½ teaspoon vanilla extract

Pinch of salt

Handful of ice

**switch it up**
Feel free to swap out the hazelnut butter for your favorite nut or seed butter. Tahini, peanut butter, almond butter, or cashew butter all produce equally delicious results!

Something about creating an açai bowl makes you feel accomplished, like you just finished a hot yoga class before 9:00 a.m. It could be the exotic and beautiful açai (pronounced *ah-sah-ee*) berry, or the fact that you're boosting your glow from the inside out. Whatever it is, I'm here for it because açai bowls are also incredibly delicious and refreshing. The addition of hemp seeds and collagen to this recipe offers healthy fats and protein to keep you satiated all morning. Serve with your favorite granola for a satisfying cool-crunchy bite.

# adaptogenic açai smoothie bowl

**makes 1 smoothie bowl**

1 cup coconut water or water, plus more as needed

¾ cup frozen mixed berries (blueberries, blackberries, raspberries, strawberries)

1 frozen banana, peeled and sliced

1 (3.5-ounce/100g) package frozen açai (see page 26)

1 tablespoon hemp seeds

1 tablespoon goji berries

1 tablespoon collagen powder (optional)

Granola, fresh fruit, nut butter, bee pollen, and/or coconut chips, for serving (optional)

In a high-speed blender, combine the coconut water, mixed berries, banana, açai, hemp seeds, goji berries, and collagen (if using).

Blend for 45 to 60 seconds, adding more coconut water or stopping to scrape down the sides as needed, until a creamy consistency has been reached (it should look a bit like soft-serve ice cream). If your blender is giving you trouble, just add more coconut water and make it a smoothie instead of a bowl.

Pour the mixture into your cutest bowl and serve with any or all of the suggested toppings. Dig in.

Often the best recipes aren't technically recipes at all. This yogurt bowl is a reminder that sometimes we just need to skip the fussy breakfast and make a delicious yogurt bowl with things we have on hand. Gut-loving yogurt, paired with fiber-packed toppers like hemp seeds, chia, and berries, make this a super-satisfying start to the day. When I prepare this, I like to imagine I'm at an ice cream sundae bar, and I go a little heavy-handed on the granola and honey.

# superfruit yogurt bowl

To your favorite bowl, add the yogurt and berries.

Top with the granola, goji berries, hemp seeds, chia seeds, and bee pollen. Drizzle with the honey and serve.

**makes 1 bowl**

½ cup plain Greek or coconut yogurt

¼ cup fresh or frozen berries

2 to 3 tablespoons Salted Caramel Cashew Granola (page 82) or your favorite granola

1 tablespoon goji berries (see page 29)

1 teaspoon hemp seeds

1 teaspoon chia seeds

1 teaspoon bee pollen (see page 26)

1 to 2 teaspoons raw honey or maple syrup

Meet my beauty, my pride and joy. I have made this granola hundreds of times and don't plan on trying a new recipe anytime soon. The "salted caramel" vibe comes from the maple syrup and kiss of sea salt. Ghee is a favorite fat here, adding to the intoxicating buttery aroma, but coconut oil won't steer you wrong either. Don't do what I did my first three times making granola and forget to keep an eye on it in the oven—you want this nutty granola deeply tanned but not blackened.

# salted caramel cashew granola

### makes about 3 cups

2 cups old-fashioned oats

½ cup raw cashews, coarsely chopped

⅓ cup raw almonds, coarsely chopped

1½ tablespoons maca powder (optional)

½ teaspoon ground cinnamon

½ cup ghee, butter, or coconut oil (see page 28)

⅓ cup plus 1 tablespoon maple syrup

1 tablespoon vanilla extract

½ teaspoon salt

Preheat the oven to 300°F. Line a baking sheet with parchment paper. In a large bowl, combine the oats, cashews, almonds, maca (if using), and cinnamon, and stir.

In a small saucepan, melt the ghee over medium heat. Stir in the maple syrup, vanilla, and salt.

Pour the ghee mixture over the oat mixture. Stir well to combine and then, using your hands, massage the liquid mixture into the oats.

Spread the oats onto the prepared baking sheet in an even layer. Bake for 45 to 60 minutes, stirring every 20 minutes, until the granola is golden and crisp.

Let cool completely and transfer to an airtight container. The granola will keep at room temperature for 2 to 3 weeks. (For extra-crisp granola, store it in the refrigerator.) Crunch and enjoy.

What are your thoughts on dessert for breakfast? When it's packed with gut-loving fiber and healthy fats and still manages to be delicious, I tend to be on board. This combination of creamy coconut milk and rich raw cacao makes for a super-craveable chia pudding that is, dare I say . . . almost like brownie batter. Crown the pudding with granola and berries and you've become #brunchgoals. Canned full-fat coconut milk produces the best flavor and mouthfeel for this chia pudding, but your favorite plant milk will also work just fine.

# brownie batter chia pudding

In a medium-sized jar or bowl, combine the coconut milk, water, cacao, 1 tablespoon of the maple syrup, the vanilla, chaga (if using), and salt. Whisk well. Stir in the chia seeds. Taste and add the remaining 1 tablespoon maple syrup if necessary.

Cover and refrigerate for at least 3 hours or overnight, until the chia seeds have absorbed the liquid and the mixture has a pudding-like consistency. (If the mixture is thicker than desired, stir in a splash of water or milk.)

Serve with any or all of the suggested toppings.

**makes 2 servings**

1 cup canned full-fat coconut milk, plus more as needed

½ cup water

1 tablespoon raw cacao powder

1 to 2 tablespoons maple syrup

¾ teaspoon vanilla extract

¾ teaspoon chaga powder (optional)

Pinch of salt

3 tablespoons chia seeds (see page 28)

Granola, toasted coconut flakes, strawberries, and/ or raspberries, for serving (optional)

There's not much that can't benefit from a dollop of strawberry compote. Boring oatmeal? Add some compote. Almond butter toast? Compote. Sad bowl of plain yogurt? Compote. You see where I'm going with this. If you were wondering, *compote* is just a fancy word for fruit sauce. To make our beautiful fruit sauce nice and jelly-like, you don't need heaps of sugar or gelatin—just add chia! Chia seeds plump up to make this sauce shockingly jam-like, the perfect consistency for compote.

# strawberry sunshine chia compote

**makes about 1¼ cups**

2 cups strawberries, sliced

½ cup water

1½ tablespoons chia seeds (see page 28)

1 to 2 teaspoons raw honey

1 teaspoon orange zest

Pinch of salt

In a medium saucepan, combine the strawberries and water. Cover and cook on medium heat for 10 to 12 minutes, stirring occasionally, until the strawberries have softened. Use a spatula or wooden spoon to crush the strawberries into a chunky sauce.

Stir in the chia seeds, honey, orange zest, and salt. Cook for 1 to 2 more minutes, until thickened slightly. Remove from the heat and let cool completely. Transfer to an airtight container. The compote will keep, refrigerated, for up to 4 days.

The glutton in me is always looking to make healthy things taste like crave-worthy treats. In my experience dabbling in the healthy breakfast world, overnight oats have a high probability of tasting like glue. Naturally, I had to do something about this. Creamy plant-based milk with cinnamon and maple syrup is a worthy base for these oats, with ribbons of almond butter swirled in at the end. A fruity compote is my secret weapon for making any oatmeal taste exceptional; you can use the Strawberry Sunshine Chia Compote, fresh berries, or any favorite low-sugar jams you have on hand.

# almond butter & jam overnight oats

In a jar or bowl, combine all the ingredients except the almond butter and compote. Taste and add more sweetness if needed. Add the almond butter and stir gently, leaving some swirls intact.

Refrigerate for at least 2 hours or overnight, until the chia seeds have plumped.

Serve with any or all of the suggested toppings.

**makes 1 generous serving**

⅓ cup oats (quick-cooking or old-fashioned)

2 teaspoons chia seeds (see page 28)

⅓ cup plant-based milk

⅓ cup water

1 tablespoon maple syrup

Pinch of ground cinnamon

Pinch of salt

1 tablespoon almond butter

Strawberry Sunshine Chia Compote (page 86), strawberry jam, fresh berries, coconut yogurt, and/or granola, for serving (optional)

Have you hopped on the savory oatmeal train yet? Simple, nutritious, and satisfying, savory oats feel like a quick-cooking risotto that you get to indulge in at breakfast time (heck yes to that!). If you're like me and always trying to get more veggies into your day, these oats are a delicious vehicle for them. I like to use a mixture of broth and water for the cooking liquid, which makes for flavorful (but not overly salty) oats.

# savory miso oatmeal with green onions

### makes 2 servings

1 tablespoon coconut oil, ghee, or butter

¾ cup quick-cooking oats

2 green onions, thinly sliced, divided

2 cups water, bone broth, or vegetable broth (or a combination)

1 tablespoon white miso paste

Salt and freshly ground black pepper

Soft-boiled eggs, toasted sesame seeds, sriracha, and/or tamari, for serving (optional)

In a medium saucepan, combine the coconut oil, oats, and half of the green onions. Cook over medium heat for 3 to 4 minutes, until the oats are aromatic and take on a bit of color.

Add the water and bring to a simmer over medium-high heat.

Reduce the heat to medium-low. Cover and cook for 8 to 12 minutes, stirring occasionally, until the mixture is creamy and most of the water has been absorbed.

Stir in the miso until it dissolves. Taste and season with salt and pepper if needed. Serve immediately with the remaining green onions and any or all of the suggested toppings.

### customize it

Extra veggies hanging around your fridge or freezer? Give them a quick sauté and add them in to bolster your savory porridge. Cauliflower, mushrooms, spinach, and frozen peas are a few of my faves to stir in for extra nutrients and fiber.

Hear me out: there's *no* reason your oatmeal breakfast shouldn't taste as good as a warm tray of cinnamon rolls. This version leans heavy into the cinnamon roll flavor profile (you're welcome), with hints of cozy chai spices. It tastes like bakery decadence and smells like pure heaven.

# chai cinnamon roll baked oatmeal

### makes 4 to 6 servings

2 cups oats (quick-cooking or old-fashioned)

1 teaspoon baking powder

½ teaspoon salt

2 teaspoons ground cinnamon (see page 28)

½ teaspoon ground ginger

½ teaspoon ground cardamom

¼ teaspoon nutmeg

2 large eggs

2 cups plant-based milk

⅓ cup maple syrup

¼ cup ghee or coconut oil, melted

1 teaspoon vanilla extract

½ cup coarsely chopped pecans

Maple syrup or Salted Tahini "Caramel" (page 180), for serving (optional)

Preheat the oven to 350°F. Line a 9 by 9-inch baking dish or skillet with parchment paper.

In a large bowl, combine the oats, baking powder, salt, cinnamon, ginger, cardamom, and nutmeg. Whisk to combine. In a second large bowl, combine the eggs, milk, maple syrup, ghee, and vanilla. Whisk well. Pour the dry mixture into the bowl with the wet ingredients and whisk until a smooth batter forms.

Pour the oat mixture into the prepared baking dish and sprinkle with the pecans. Let the mixture sit for 5 minutes.

Bake for 35 to 40 minutes, until firm and cooked throughout.

Serve right away as is, or with a drizzle of maple syrup or Salted Tahini Caramel if desired. Any leftovers will keep, refrigerated, for 4 to 6 days.

**customize it**

This recipe makes a generous family-sized portion of baked oats. If you live alone, or with an oat-hater like I do, you can halve the recipe easily for 2 or 3 portions.

# good vibes all day

Whatever journey we are on in life, days can get busy and stressful, often causing us to put self-care on the bottom of our to-do list (if at all). The ritual of making nourishing tonics and elixirs is a great way to check in with your mind and body midday and say, "I'm thinking of you." Sometimes, I'm tonic-ing to stay grounded amidst an eventful day (Lime Ginger-Aid, page 100). Other times, I'll whip up something high-energy to spark a little fire and inspiration (Matcha Energy Soda, page 108). No matter how your day is going, it's a wonderful thing to be able to slow down and take a moment to create something that will make you feel cared for. These daytime tonics are high on hydration and energy to keep you going (and glowing!) all day long.

# ten ways to feel good right now

We all get stuck in a bad-mood spiral occasionally. Sometimes tough things are happening behind the scenes, we're on edge after a stressful week at work, or we're feeling tired or uninspired for no apparent reason at all (my personal favorite). Building a roster of habits to remedy these moments can help shorten a bad week into a bad day. Here are a few of my favorite ways to move through negative energy and get started on a path that serves you better.

### Do some deep breathing

Take a minute, slow down your breathing, and tune in to your body. By breathing more slowly and more deeply, you release endorphins and nudge your nervous system to calm down.

### Make a mood-boosting tonic

Instead of reaching for another cup of coffee or a sugary snack, bridge the afternoon with an uplifting elixir. Some of my favorite tonics for an improved mood are the Sexy Superfood Hot Cacao (page 140), Chocolate Mood Mylk (page 111), and Good Mood Iced Matcha Latte (page 112).

### Step outside for a walk

The simple act of moving your two feet can boost endorphins, reduce stress hormones, and help balance your mood. It only takes a few minutes to change up your scenery, freshen your perspective, and increase the blood flow to your brain and body.

### Cook something nourishing

When I am stressed or feeling low, I put my energy into creating a bountiful grain bowl with greens, veggies, and a delicious dressing, like the Hydrating Spring Roll Salad (page 118). My belly is full, my body is happy, and my mind is satisfied.

## Practice positive affirmations

Create your own personal power mantras to speak and write out when you need a boost. Some of my own favorites: "I am grateful to attract abundance and joy," "I am enough as I am," and "I am grateful to complete my workday with ease and fun."

## Use music therapy

Play an upbeat song that brings you joy. Create a playlist that curates all your longtime favorites (no judgment if it's purely ABBA or early-2000s pop). In my house there's nothing that dancing to Beyoncé's "Flawless" can't fix.

## Make someone else's day

Nothing feels as gratifying as giving! Send a note expressing your appreciation or complimenting someone you care for—a partner, a parent, or an old friend.

## Look at how far you've come

We can get caught up in all that we are not, without appreciating all that we are. Look back and take note of how proud you are of yourself for overcoming a challenge, for your bravery in trying new things, or for dusting yourself off after a fall.

## Switch your perspective

Sometimes we get caught up in the "have-tos" and lose appreciation for our daily routine. Try switching out "I *have* to finish this project for work" with "I *get* the privilege to work on a challenging project that improves my skills and provides for me."

## Set small goals

Tackling big goals all at once can be overwhelming; break up your big shiny aspirations into smaller chunks. The satisfaction of checking off a goal, no matter how small, can produce momentum and inspire a feeling of "I've got this!"

This gorgeously hued hydrator is a Lake & Oak community favorite, for good reason. Not only is it radically refreshing, but it's packed with antioxidants and nutrients that bolster immunity and protect your summer skin. Any hibiscus tea blend will work great here, but you'll find the hibiscus-rosehip combination available at most grocers and health-food stores. The collagen is optional but boosts the glow benefits and produces a pretty frothy effect when everything is shaken together.

# hibiscus beauty tonic

To a heatproof vessel, add the tea bags and pour the boiling water over them. Let steep, covered, for 10 minutes (or as long as you can stand to wait). Remove the tea bags (strain the tea leaves if using loose tea).

In a jar or shaker, combine the steeped tea, lime juice, maple syrup, and collagen (if using). Shake well for 10 to 20 seconds, until frothy and combined.

Fill a glass with ice and pour the tea mixture over the ice. Garnish with any of the suggested toppings. Sip and soak up the vibrant goodness.

**makes 1 tonic**

2 tea bags or 1 tablespoon loose-leaf hibiscus-rosehip tea

1 cup boiling water

Juice of ½ lime

2 teaspoons maple syrup or raw honey

1 tablespoon collagen powder (optional; see page 29)

Sliced cucumber, fresh mint leaves, and/or rose petals, for topping (optional)

Healthy "booster shots" are popular but often come with a steep price tag. So let's make our own! Freshly squeezed orange juice is kicked up with ginger and turmeric for antioxidants and immunity-revving power. Serve straight-up or dilute with sparkling water for a golden mocktail.

# flu-fighter wellness shots

### makes 2 shots

Juice of 1 large orange

Juice of 1 large lemon

½ teaspoon ground turmeric

½ teaspoon ground ginger

Pinch of cayenne pepper

To a glass jar with a lid or a shaker, add all of the ingredients. Shake well to combine.

Pour into a glass. Pucker up and enjoy!

### switch it up

Swap out ground turmeric and ginger for 1 teaspoon each of freshly grated turmeric and ginger.

I was first introduced to this refreshing tonic while traveling in southern India. We sipped it riverside in Kerala while feasting on papadum and thali. I like to keep a knob of fresh ginger handy and whip this together whenever bloating or a bellyache hits. With soothing ginger and cooling lime, it's the perfect complement to a rich and spicy meal.

# lime ginger-aid

### makes 1 tonic

1 tablespoon fresh lime juice

1 teaspoon finely grated fresh ginger (see page 29)

1 teaspoon maple syrup

1 cup sparkling or flat water

In your favorite glass, combine the lime juice, ginger, and maple syrup. Top with the water. Add ice if desired. Stir gently, sip, and enjoy.

When I was in the thick of my nutrition program, I felt it was a rite of passage to equip my tiny condo kitchen with a top-of-the-line cold-press juicer. After getting more juice and pulp on the walls of my kitchen than in the glass, I retired that juicer and became strictly a blender girl. This refreshing green drink celebrates cucumber, a mega-hydrating skin food that blends up effortlessly into this highly sippable tonic. Spiked with lime and fresh mint, it tastes like a day at the spa.

# cucumber mint hydrator

**makes 2 to 4 drinks**

2 cups water

2 medium cucumbers, cut into 2-inch pieces (about 2 cups), plus thin slices for garnish

4 to 6 fresh mint leaves

Juice of 1 lime

1 to 2 tablespoons maple syrup or raw honey, plus more as needed

Pinch of salt

In a high-speed blender, combine all the ingredients. Blend for 40 to 60 seconds, until smooth and well combined. Strain the mixture through a fine-mesh sieve into a wide-mouthed pitcher or bowl. Taste and add more sweetener if desired.

Serve over ice with a slice of cucumber on top. Enjoy right away, or keep refrigerated in a jar or airtight container for up to 3 days.

---

**customize it**

This tonic is great for making in large batches and serving to a very appreciative crowd. Make ahead and double or triple the recipe. Celebrating? Make it a low-ABV cocktail with a splash of gin or vodka.

Commonly enjoyed in Mexico and Central America, agua fresca is a divine creation of fruit blended with water into a refreshing beverage. Sign me up for that! This recipe uses super-hydrating watermelon and lime juice, which fuse into a sweet and tangy summer dream. Chia seeds are added for their fun jelly texture and benefits; the insoluble fiber they contain acts like a digestive broom for your insides. Cheers to a hydrated body and happy belly!

# watermelon chia agua fresca

To a high-speed blender, add the watermelon. Blend for 30 seconds, until the watermelon is broken down and a smooth liquid has formed. Stir in the lime juice, chia seeds, and salt. Refrigerate for at least 1 hour, or until the chia have plumped. Keep refrigerated in a jar or airtight container for up to 3 days.

**makes 2 drinks**

5 cups coarsely chopped seeded ripe watermelon

Juice of 1 lime

1½ tablespoons chia seeds (see page 28)

Pinch of salt

**customize it**

For a smoother, less fibrous beverage, after blending, use a fine-mesh sieve to strain the watermelon mixture into a large bowl or pitcher.

No juice bar is complete without a signature detox tonic, often colored with dark and mystical activated charcoal or other hard-to-pronounce superfood ingredients. If I owned a juice bar, this would be my version: a mix of refreshing lemongrass iced tea, zingy lime, and a hint of sweetness to balance it out. If you're wary of the charcoal addition or don't have it on hand, this tonic is still incredibly sippable without.

# charcoal lemongrass limeade

### makes 1 tonic

2 lemongrass tea bags or 1 tablespoon dried lemongrass

¾ cup boiling water

1 tablespoon maple syrup or raw honey

Juice of ½ lime

¼ teaspoon food-grade activated charcoal (optional; see page 26)

Fresh mint for garnish (optional)

To your favorite heatproof glass, add the tea bags and pour the boiling water over. Cover and steep for 10 minutes (or as long as you can stand to wait). Remove the tea bags (or strain the tea) and stir in the maple syrup, lime juice, and charcoal (if using). Top with 2 cups of ice to cool instantly, and garnish with mint if desired. Sip and revitalize!

Skip the canned energy drinks and whip up this energizing and mood-bolstering matcha when you need a pick-me-up. The simple combination of sparkling water, matcha, and lemon gives you a refreshing boost of hydration, antioxidants, *and* caffeine (take that, iced coffee!).

# matcha energy soda

### makes 1 soda

1 (12-ounce/355ml) can unflavored sparkling water

Handful of ice

¾ teaspoon matcha powder

1 teaspoon maple syrup

Juice of ¼ lemon or lime

Citrus wedge, for garnish (optional)

To a tall glass, add the sparkling water and ice. In a small bowl, combine the matcha powder, maple syrup, and lemon juice. Whisk in a zigzag pattern for about 15 seconds, until foamy.

Slowly pour the matcha mixture over the soda (it can bubble over if you pour too fast). Garnish with the citrus wedge if desired. Sip and energize.

### switch it up

Keep it interesting by alternating your sparkling water flavors. Strawberry, passion fruit, and coconut pair deliciously with the savory notes of matcha.

Growing up in the '90s, drinking icy-cold chocolate milk straight from the carton was as satisfying as it got. This super-food version uses bliss-boosting raw cacao and reishi for a nutty, chocolatey flavor. It tastes like gourmet chocolate milk and feels like a happy dance in your brain. Serve it over ice and bring on the endorphins!

# chocolate mood mylk

To a high-speed blender, add all the ingredients. Blend for 60 to 90 seconds, until frothy and smooth. Enjoy as is, or (my personal favorite) pour over ice.

Store in a jar or airtight container in the refrigerator for 2 to 4 days.

## makes about 2 cups

½ cup hemp seeds

2 cups warm water

3 tablespoons raw cacao powder

2 to 3 tablespoons maple syrup

½ teaspoon vanilla extract

½ teaspoon reishi powder

¼ teaspoon salt

Pinch of ground cinnamon (optional)

Pinch of nutmeg (optional)

### customize it
This recipe leaves lots of room for improvisation. Add more water for a lighter, thinner milk, or less, for a cream-like consistency. Add peanut butter for a nutty twist, or boost the spices with cayenne or chipotle for a Mexican-inspired chocolate drink.

I didn't dream up the combo of juicy strawberries and earthy matcha, but I'm glad someone did. My version of this head-turning drink uses homemade strawberry milk for a decadent creamy base. Matcha tea is packed with L-theanine, sure to keep your vibe high all afternoon.

# strawberry matcha latte

**makes 1 latte**

1 cup Strawberry Dream Milk (page 48)

1 teaspoon matcha powder (see page 32)

1 teaspoon raw honey or maple syrup

1 tablespoon water

Fill your favorite tall glass with ice and add the strawberry milk.

In a small bowl, combine the matcha, honey, and water. Whisk in a zigzag pattern for about 15 seconds, until foamy. Slowly pour the matcha mixture over the milk. Stir gently, sip, and bliss out.

My first iced matcha latte was at Cha Matcha in New York. The walls were neon pink and the matcha a gorgeous green—it was heaven! Here, you can have your own matcha bliss, without the high price tag and plastic cup.

# good mood iced matcha latte

**makes 1 latte**

1 teaspoon matcha powder

1 to 2 teaspoons raw honey

¼ teaspoon vanilla extract

¼ teaspoon maca powder

1 cup ice cubes

1 cup oat milk

CBD oil, dosage according to package directions (optional)

To your favorite glass, add the matcha, honey, vanilla, maca, and a splash of water. Whisk in a zigzag pattern for about 15 seconds, until foamy.

Top with the ice, oat milk, and CBD (if using). Stir, sip, and bliss out.

Traditional Japanese ramen is a labor of love, with the result being nothing short of life-changing goodness in a bowl. To satisfy my craving for ramen and compensate for my lack of time (and patience), I developed this streamlined version of the umami-packed noodles. When serving for friends and family, I get a lot of "oooohs," but I never tell how quick and simple it was to make. It also happens to be teeming with anti-inflammatory ingredients that your insides will high-five you for.

# fifteen-minute immunity ramen

In a large pot, combine the broth, ginger, garlic, and half of the green onions. Bring to a boil over medium-high heat. Cover and reduce heat to medium-low. Cook for 5 to 6 minutes, until aromatic.

Add the miso, tahini, and tamari, whisking well to combine. Stir in the spinach and remove the pot from the heat (the residual heat will cook the spinach). Taste and add more tamari, if needed.

Divide the noodles between two bowls, then ladle the broth and aromatics over top. Garnish with the remaining green onions and any other desired toppings. Serve immediately.

**makes 2 servings**

4 cups vegetable or chicken broth

1 tablespoon finely grated fresh ginger

2 garlic cloves, thinly sliced

3 green onions, light green and white parts, thinly sliced, divided

2 tablespoons white miso paste (see page 32)

2 tablespoons tahini

1 tablespoon tamari or coconut aminos, plus more as needed

2 cups coarsely chopped baby spinach or kale

2 (5-ounce/140g) packages brown rice ramen noodles, cooked according to package directions, drained, and kept warm

Tamari, toasted sesame oil, red pepper flakes, soft-boiled eggs, and/ or chopped cilantro, for topping (optional)

Despite its humble ingredients, this golden soup packs a flavor punch, thanks to a symphony of garlic, lemon, and warming turmeric. The plant protein from chickpeas, quinoa, and greens will satisfy even the strongest tummy rumbles. I imagine it on the menu as part of a vibrant spring "refresh" or to help bolster immunity in January.

# life-affirming chickpea soup

### makes 2 or 3 servings

1 tablespoon coconut oil, ghee, or olive oil

1 yellow onion, finely chopped

4 garlic cloves, thinly sliced

1 tablespoon finely chopped fresh ginger

1 (15-ounce/425g) can chickpeas, drained and liquid reserved

1¼ teaspoons curry powder

¼ teaspoon ground turmeric

1 teaspoon salt, plus more as needed

Pinch of red pepper flakes (optional)

Freshly ground black pepper

4 cups low-sodium vegetable or chicken broth

¼ cup uncooked white quinoa, rinsed

2 cups baby arugula or spinach, coarsely chopped

Zest and juice of 1 lemon, divided

In a large pot, heat the coconut oil over medium heat.

Add the onion, garlic, and ginger. Cook for 4 to 5 minutes over medium-low heat, stirring occasionally, until tender. Add the drained chickpeas, curry powder, turmeric, salt, and red pepper flakes (if using). Season with black pepper.

Cook for 3 to 4 minutes over medium heat, stirring often. Use a spatula or wooden spoon to smash some of the chickpeas into the pot (this gives the soup a lovely chunky texture).

Add the broth, quinoa, and reserved chickpea liquid. Bring to a simmer over medium-high heat. Once it's simmering, reduce the heat to medium-low. Cover and cook for 13 to 15 minutes, until the quinoa is cooked and the soup has thickened.

Stir in the arugula, lemon zest, and half of the lemon juice. Taste and add more salt, pepper, or lemon juice as desired. Grab a spoon and tuck in!

I've made this rainbow number dozens of times—for Mother's Day picnics, birthdays, workdays, and summers by the lake. Its superpower lies in being both satisfying and energizing, healthy and crazy-delicious. Don't fuss over finding the exact ingredients listed here; the recipe is adaptable to whatever's in season or in your kitchen. Just don't skip the dressing!

# hydrating spring roll salad

## makes 2 servings

1 (2.8-ounce/79g) bundle uncooked soba noodles

1 teaspoon toasted sesame oil

1 heaping cup thinly sliced green or red cabbage

1 heaping cup thinly sliced romaine lettuce

⅓ English cucumber, halved lengthwise and thinly sliced

½ red bell pepper, thinly sliced

4 to 6 basil leaves, finely chopped

¼ cup finely chopped cilantro

4 to 6 mint leaves, finely chopped

¼ cup coarsely chopped cashews

¼ cup Sweet Sesame Ginger Dressing (page 180)

Sliced watermelon radish, toasted sesame seeds, and/or toasted coconut flakes, for topping (optional)

Cook the noodles according to package directions. Drain and rinse with cool water. Drizzle with the sesame oil.

In your favorite shallow bowl, arrange half of the cabbage, romaine, cucumber, bell pepper, and noodles in separate sections for a visual treat. Sprinkle half of the basil, cilantro, mint, and cashews over the top. Drizzle with half of the dressing. Serve with any of the suggested toppings if desired. Repeat with a second bowl. Admire your work and enjoy.

This gratifying soup will load you up with a hearty dose of greens without making you feel like you're on day one of a liquid cleanse. Sautéed broccoli and onions add a depth of flavor to the broth, with cashews and nutritional yeast giving a nod to glorious cream-of-broccoli soup. It's so creamy and unctuous, you'll be shocked there's not a shred of Parmesan or drop of cream in sight.

# super green soup

In a large pot, warm the coconut oil over medium heat. Add the onion, garlic, and broccoli. Cook for 8 to 10 minutes, stirring occasionally, until the onion is golden and slightly tender.

Add the broth, cashews, nutritional yeast, smoked paprika, red pepper flakes, and salt. Season with black pepper. Bring to a boil. Reduce the heat to low and simmer, covered, for 8 to 10 minutes, until the broccoli is tender.

Off the heat, stir in the spinach and lemon juice. Let cool for 5 minutes. Transfer to a high-speed blender, working in batches if necessary and blend for 45 to 60 seconds, until smooth and creamy. Taste and adjust seasonings as necessary. Garnish with more pepper flakes and a dollop of yogurt or a drizzle of coconut milk, if you like, and serve.

**makes 2 to 4 servings**

1½ tablespoons coconut oil

1 yellow onion,
finely chopped

4 garlic cloves,
coarsely chopped

1 pound (400g) broccoli
stems and florets,
cut into 1-inch pieces
(about 6 cups)

5 cups vegetable or
chicken broth

⅓ cup raw cashews

3 tablespoons
nutritional yeast
(see page 32)

¼ teaspoon smoked paprika

¼ teaspoon red pepper
flakes, plus more for serving

¾ teaspoon salt, plus more
as needed

Freshly ground black pepper

2 cups baby spinach

Juice of ¼ lemon

Plain yogurt or coconut
milk, for serving (optional)

Cooking up a pot of this Indian-style dal feels like slipping on a pair of well-worn jeans. It's familiar, it's comfortable, and yet it still looks like you tried. Traditional Indian ingredients like turmeric, ginger, and coconut milk are abundant in this recipe, playing double duty with their incredible flavor and health-promoting properties.

# restorative golden dal

In a large pot, warm the ghee over medium-high heat. Add the onion and cauliflower. Reduce the heat to medium-low and cook for 6 to 8 minutes, stirring occasionally, until the vegetables are tender and slightly golden.

Add the tomato paste, ginger, garlic, and spices. Cook for 3 to 4 minutes, stirring often, until the spices are toasted and aromatic. Add the broth, lentils, and coconut milk and bring to a boil. Stir in the salt and add pepper to taste.

Reduce the heat to medium-low, cover, and simmer for 13 to 15 minutes, stirring occasionally, until the lentils are tender and the liquid is absorbed. Taste and adjust the seasonings as needed.

Serve in bowls with any of the suggested toppings (see Customize It, below). Store any leftovers, refrigerated, for 4 to 6 days.

**makes 4 servings**

1 tablespoon ghee, butter, or coconut oil

1 yellow onion, finely chopped

2 cups cauliflower, cut into small florets

2 tablespoons tomato paste

1 teaspoon minced fresh ginger

2 garlic cloves, finely chopped

1 tablespoon curry powder

1 teaspoon ground cumin

½ teaspoon ground coriander

½ teaspoon garam masala

½ teaspoon ground turmeric (see page 33)

3 cups vegetable broth, chicken broth, or water

1 cup dried red lentils

1 (14-ounce/414ml) can full-fat coconut milk

¾ teaspoon salt, plus more as needed

Freshly ground black pepper

## customize it
Top with yogurt and red pepper flakes or a pinch of fresh herbs like cilantro or sprouts. Serve with naan and/or steamed basmati rice.

Picture this: it's 3:00 p.m. on a Tuesday, and your energy and motivation have dipped. You don't want a coffee, but you could definitely use a boost. That's where these energy bites come in—nourishing, wholesome, and dangerously truffle-like. Cacao, almonds, and hemp seeds are great sources of magnesium and tryptophan, which are known to relax the mind and contribute to higher levels of serotonin (aka the happy hormone).

# chocolate hazelnut energy bites

**makes 10 to 15 energy bites**

1¼ cups raw hazelnuts

6 Medjool dates, pitted (see page 32)

2 tablespoons hemp seeds

2½ tablespoons raw cacao powder

2 tablespoons hazelnut or almond butter

2 teaspoons cordyceps powder (optional)

1 tablespoon maple syrup (optional)

Pinch of salt

Preheat the oven to 350°F. Line a baking sheet with parchment paper. Add the hazelnuts to the sheet and bake for 10 minutes, until lightly toasted. Let cool slightly.

In a small bowl, soak the dates in hot water for 5 minutes, until softened slightly. Drain and set aside.

Use a damp paper towel to rub the nuts and remove as many of the dark brown skins as possible (I usually get about half off). Transfer the nuts to a food processor. Pulse for 20 to 30 seconds, until finely chopped. Scoop out about ⅓ cup and set aside.

Add the dates and all the remaining ingredients to the processor and pulse for 30 to 40 seconds, until a rough "dough" starts to form. Add 1 to 2 tablespoons water to assist blending as needed.

Spread the reserved chopped hazelnuts on a work surface. Form the date mixture into 1- to 2-inch balls, and roll them in the hazelnuts to cover all sides. Enjoy right away or refrigerate in an airtight container for 2 to 3 weeks. They'll keep in the freezer for up to 3 months.

# golden hour

The sexiest time of day. The sun is setting and you're plotting closing your laptop and curling up on the couch or heading out for a night of fun. During this sacred hour, I'm cutting caffeine and sipping on something cozy like the Sexy Superfood Hot Cacao (page 140) or festive like the Spicy Grapefruit Detox Margarita (page 143). Whether you're hibernating, celebrating, or anything in between—there's a tonic for that.

# seven ways to wind down from your day

Many of us hold onto a lot of stress during the day from our jobs, families, and never-ending to-do lists. I like to find time on weekday evenings to partake in self-care to sustain my energy and regain a bit of balance. Whether you have three hours or thirty minutes for yourself in the evenings, these are a few of my favorite ways to shake off the day and reset for a relaxed night.

## Get into comfy clothing

Change your outfit, change your mood! This is especially helpful if you work from home and have a hard time separating work from personal life. Changing into designated "rest clothing" after your workday can signal your brain that it's time to chill and set the tone for a more relaxed evening.

## Get physical

Admittedly not as fun or easy as putting on a pair of soft sweats but just as effective! Instead of parking in front of the TV right away, I like to make a habit of scheduling a yoga class or workout to kick off the evening. I may go into the workout feeling frustrated or overwhelmed, but I come out with a fresh boost of endorphins, feeling satisfied from an hour well spent.

## Take a bath or shower

Your shower is good for more than getting you clean! The act of a warm bath or shower can be therapeutic, as it naturally relaxes your muscles, slows your thoughts, and gives you a break from your busy schedule. Take it a step further and use it as an opportunity to slow down and practice gratitude, or lather up with a spa-worthy body scrub.

## Plan a "play" date with yourself

To spice up your weekday evenings, carve out some time to try something new, or do something playful that you enjoy. Watercolor classes? Surf lessons? Checking out a new local shop? Trying new things can increase creativity, reduce stress, and build self-esteem.

## Shake up an evening tonic

Wind down without the wine! Treat yourself and make the evening feel special with a delicious and healthy tonic that suits your mood. Break out the cocktail glasses, get comfy, and soak up a little me time. I love to whip up the Hibiscus Beauty Tonic (page 99) to rehydrate and unwind post-yoga.

## Put the phone down

One of the most impactful things I *try* to do for myself is to put my phone and laptop away in the evening. When I am not stressing out over my inbox or scrolling social media, I'm living more in the present moment, and my sleep quality improves. Give it a try for a few hours one evening and enjoy a bit of luxurious tech-free living!

## Be kind to yourself

Above all, listen to your body and honor what it needs. Craving friendship or community? Reach out to a pal or loved one. Overwhelmed? Opt out of plans if possible and take the night off to restore. When things get tough, we have a habit of being hard on ourselves, instead of giving ourselves some well-deserved TLC.

Over the past few years, our collective obsession with seltzer, soda, and sparkling water has hit an all-time high. I'm right on the bandwagon, often filling my shopping cart with a rainbow of different brands, flavors, and benefits. I developed this ginger soda when I wanted a fun and health-promoting way to enjoy plain sparkling water at home. The turmeric ginger syrup is very simple to whip up, lasts ages in the fridge, and makes for an incredibly satisfying health-ified soda. Think of this tonic as a ginger kombucha without the puckery tang!

# sparkling turmeric ginger soda

### makes 1 soda

1¼ cups unflavored sparkling water

2 tablespoons Turmeric Ginger Syrup (recipe follows)

1 lemon wedge

1 lemon wheel, for serving (optional)

To your favorite glass, add the sparkling water. Slowly pour in the Turmeric Ginger Syrup (it can bubble over if you pour too fast). Squeeze the lemon wedge into the drink.

Gently stir, and place a lemon wheel on the rim of the glass if desired. Serve immediately and soak up the golden glow!

## turmeric ginger syrup

### makes about 1 cup

1½ cups chopped fresh ginger (skin-on is fine)

1 teaspoon ground turmeric or 2 tablespoons chopped fresh turmeric (skin-on is fine)

2 cups water

½ cup raw honey

In a medium saucepan, combine the ginger, turmeric, and water. Bring to a simmer over medium-high heat. Once it's simmering, reduce the heat to low and cook for 25 minutes, until reduced by about half.

Strain the mixture through a fine-mesh sieve into a medium-sized bowl. Add the honey and whisk well to combine. Store in an airtight container in the refrigerator for up to 1 month.

**switch it up**

If you're not a soda freak like me, Turmeric Ginger Syrup makes for a tasty instant tea when paired with hot water. Start with 1 to 2 tablespoons of syrup per cup of water and add more for a punchier tonic.

Hydrating watermelon, superfood goji, and juicy strawberries are a match made in adult slushie heaven. Blend it up in 5 minutes or less and transport yourself poolside.

# watermelon beauty slushie

In a high-speed blender, combine all the ingredients. Blend for 30 to 60 seconds, stopping to scrape down the sides of the blender as needed.

Pour into your favorite glass, slurp, and enjoy.

**makes 2 slushies**

1 cup water or coconut water

1 cup frozen diced seeded watermelon

1 cup frozen strawberries

2 teaspoons goji berries (see page 29)

1 teaspoon raw honey (optional)

I fondly call this tonic "the broke gal's kombucha" because it gives you that hit of sour that die-hard 'booch lovers crave, at a fraction of the cost. It's not too much of a stretch because of the gut-happy benefits that make up organic raw apple cider vinegar. Start small with a tiny splash of ACV and see how you take to the tangy bite.

# love your guts spritzer

To a tall glass, add the sparkling water. Top with the apple cider vinegar. Stir gently to combine. Serve with ice if desired. Sip and enjoy the tongue-tingling goodness.

**makes 1 spritzer**

1½ cups unflavored sparkling water

1 to 2 teaspoons organic raw apple cider vinegar (see page 26)

My very first pop-up with Lake & Oak was on a scorching-hot day in June (great day to launch a tea business, I know). It was at a market on Queen Street West in Toronto, and I served up ice-cold hibiscus tonics with oversized iced tea cubes. The ice cubes were a hit and kept the drinks looking beautiful, frosty, and flavorful as they melted. I still use them today; they're great in a pitcher of iced tea and make your glass of water a lot more fun to drink!

# rose hibiscus ice cubes

In a large pitcher or glass jar, combine the hibiscus, rose petals, and cold water. Steep in the fridge for at least 5 hours or up to 2 days (for more on this method, see Cold Brew Tea on page 41).

Strain the tea mixture through a fine-mesh sieve into a wide-mouthed pitcher or bowl. Stir in the sweetener (if using) and lime juice. Pour into an ice cube tray and garnish with the remaining hibiscus and rose petals. Freeze overnight or until solid.

Add the ice cubes to your beverage, sip, and refresh!

**makes 6 to 8 large ice cubes or 32 small ice cubes**

2 tablespoons dried hibiscus leaves, plus 1 teaspoon for garnish

1 tablespoon dried rose petals, plus 1 teaspoon for garnish

4 cups cold water

2 to 3 tablespoons sweetener of your choice (optional)

Juice of ½ lime

---

**customize it**

For a faster (but slightly less flavorful) method, steep the hibiscus and rose petals in 1 cup of boiling water for 10 minutes, then add 3 cups of ice water to quickly cool the tea. Prepare the rest of the recipe as directed.

The first time I tried the combination of green juice and champagne, I was overlooking the Malibu Pier at one of my favorite brunch experiences— Malibu Farm. The air was salty, the sun was hot, and the mimosa was the perfect balance of sour, sweet, and savory. A fun, less-sweet take on the classic, this green juice mimosa pairs especially well with celebratory brunches with friends, cocktails at golden hour, and gazing at beautiful bodies of water.

# malibu green juice mimosa

### makes 1 mimosa

1 cup homemade or store-bought green juice, chilled

¼ cup dry champagne or unflavored sparkling water, chilled

To your fanciest champagne flute or cocktail glass, add the green juice. Slowly pour the champagne over. Sip and bliss out.

When I daydream of summer, I think of lazy afternoons at the lake house, cold drinks on the water, and colorful salads in the backyard. When enjoying an alfresco meal with friends and family, I like to have a pitcher of iced tea on hand to keep everyone hydrated and happy. The combination of slow-brewed green tea, juicy ripe peaches, and mint is nourishing on its own as an afternoon tonic, or you can spike it up for a special occasion with a dry white wine. For the best flavor, give the tea and peaches at least 5 hours to get acquainted—the flavors will only improve with time.

# green tea peach sangria

In a pitcher or large mason jar, combine the tea bags, mint, and peaches. Use a wooden spoon to muddle the mint and smash the peaches into small chunks.

Add the maple syrup and water. Squeeze the lemon wedge into the pitcher before dropping it in. Refrigerate for at least 5 hours or up to 2 days. Strain the mixture through a fine-mesh sieve into a wide-mouthed pitcher or bowl (discard the solids). Taste and add more sweetener if desired.

Fill 2 to 4 glasses with ice and divide the sangria among them. Top with a splash of wine if desired. Garnish with the lemon slices (if using). Sip and reenergize!

*For more on cold-brewing tea, see page 41.*

3 tea bags or 2 tablespoons loose-leaf green tea

Handful of fresh mint, plus more for garnish

2 ripe peaches, pitted and roughly chopped

2 to 4 tablespoons maple syrup or raw honey

4 cups cold water

¼ lemon wedge

Dry white wine or sparkling water, for topping (optional)

Lemon or cucumber slices, for garnish (optional)

I developed Lake & Oak's signature Cacao Mylk (a superfood hot chocolate mix) with hopes of re-creating the rich and creamy hot chocolate of my childhood (hockey skates and mini marshmallows optional). Like Cacao Mylk, this tonic is a luxurious adult take on hot cocoa that packs a soul-affirming chocolatey punch. With nature's mood-booster raw cacao and adaptogen cordyceps, I dare you not to feel good after drinking this!

# sexy superfood hot cacao

### makes 1 hot drink

1 cup plant-based milk

1 tablespoon raw cacao powder

1 to 2 teaspoons sweetener of your choice

1 teaspoon coconut oil, coconut butter, or ghee

Pinch of ground cinnamon

Pinch of salt

¾ teaspoon cordyceps powder (see page 29)

Vegan marshmallows or Dreamy Coconut Whipped Cream (page 181), for topping (optional)

In a small saucepan, combine all the ingredients. Bring to a simmer over medium-low heat. Simmer for 2 to 3 minutes, whisking well to combine. Pour into your favorite mug, add toppings if desired, and enjoy.

---

### customize it

For a frothy version, pulse the finished drink in the blender for 10 seconds, or use a hand frother until everything is combined and foamy.

The words "detox" and "margarita" likely don't belong in the same sentence, but I'm all for poking a little fun at the wild world of wellness. This vibrant margarita brings the sweet heat with freshly squeezed citrus and a little heat from cayenne (if you dare). Instead of a standard salted rim, I like a pinch of pink salt (see page 33) to emphasize the other flavors. Tequila or not, this juicy tonic is a party in a glass.

# spicy grapefruit detox margarita

In a shaker or lidded jar, combine all the ingredients with a handful of ice. Shake well to combine. Serve over ice in your favorite cocktail glass. Sip and rejoice!

### makes 1 margarita

Juice of 1 grapefruit

Juice of 1 orange

Juice of 1 lime

2 teaspoons maple syrup or raw honey

Pinch of pink Himalayan salt

Pinch of cayenne pepper (optional)

1 ounce blanco tequila or nonalcoholic spirit (optional)

Handful of ice, plus more for serving

Yes, you read that right—this tea-and-tonic queen loves a cocktail too. My favorite spirited beverages are light, gently sweetened, and packed with redeeming ingredients like fresh herbs, freshly squeezed fruits, and bold spices. Kombucha is both a wonderful mix-in for cocktails and a low-ABV alcohol stand-in on its own, thanks to its depth and puckering flavor. In this tonic, zesty ginger kombucha pairs deliciously with a squeeze of fresh lime. If you're not looking to imbibe, a splash of sparkling water and sprig of mint make for an elevated zero-proof cocktail.

# ginger kombucha mule

**makes 1 cocktail**

A few fresh mint leaves, plus more for garnish (optional)

Juice of ½ lime

1 ounce vodka, sparkling water, or alcohol-free spirit

1 cup ginger kombucha

Lime slices and fresh mint leaves, for garnish (optional)

To your favorite cocktail glass, add the mint. Muddle with a spoon or muddler, releasing some of the oils. Add the lime juice and vodka. Stir to combine.

Top with ice, then slowly add the ginger kombucha. If desired, garnish with lime and mint. Sip and be delighted!

"Nice" cream is the plant-based darling of the ice cream world: frozen sliced bananas are blended up into a shockingly convincing, scoopable icy dessert. This version channels flavors of Peppermint Patties and mint-chip ice cream, but sneaks in superfoods like cacao, chaga, and hemp seeds for a chocolatey blend with benefits.

# chaga mint chocolate "nice" cream

In a high-speed blender or food processor, combine all the ingredients except the toppings. Blend for 45 to 60 seconds, stopping often to scrape down the sides, until creamy and combined. If your blender or food processor is struggling, add a splash of milk to help move things along.

Scoop the mixture into cones or bowls and top as desired. Revel in the chocolate goodness.

## makes 2 servings

¾ cup plant-based milk, plus more as needed

2 large bananas, peeled, frozen, and sliced into ¾-inch pieces

2 tablespoons raw cacao powder (see page 27)

1 tablespoon hemp seeds

⅓ teaspoon pure peppermint extract

1 teaspoon maple syrup

1 teaspoon chaga powder (optional)

Pinch of salt

Cacao nibs, toasted coconut flakes, and/or Salted Tahini "Caramel" (page 180), for topping (optional)

## customize it

In the mood for a sippable treat? Add an extra ¾ cup plant-based milk before blending to make it a milkshake-style dessert.

This one's for the vanilla ice cream lovers and die-hard milkshake fans. Vanilla extract, vanilla almond milk, and vanilla protein powder blend together with hemp seeds and banana to create a dreamy, shake-like drink. Frozen cauliflower is my secret smoothie weapon; its flavor is undetectable, and it has a lovely creamy consistency when blended. The kid in your life (or you) won't know about the veg, but the adult will approve. Salted Caramel Cashew Granola is an optional (but heavenly) topping.

# triple vanilla shake

**makes 1 abundant smoothie**

1 cup vanilla almond milk

1 cup frozen chopped cauliflower

1 cup frozen banana pieces

¼ cup cold water

1 teaspoon vanilla extract

1 tablespoon vanilla plant-based protein powder

1 tablespoon hemp seeds (see page 31)

Salted Caramel Cashew Granola (page 82), for topping (optional)

In a high-speed blender, combine all the ingredients except the granola. Blend for 40 to 60 seconds, until smooth and creamy. Top with granola if desired.

Sip and bliss out.

This better-than-store-bought chocolate bark just may change your life. Raw cacao, coconut oil, and almond butter melt into a rich and chocolatey bite that will leave your endorphins buzzing. Have a little fun and top it with your favorite nuts or dried fruit. My personal favorite combo is a drizzle of almond butter and flaky sea salt. The added adaptogens and CBD are bonus bliss-boosters, great for PMS chocolate cravings (or any other time of the month).

# superfood chocolate bliss bark

### makes 6 to 12 pieces

⅓ cup coconut oil

3 tablespoons maple syrup

2 teaspoons almond butter, plus more for topping (optional)

⅓ cup raw cacao powder (see page 27)

1 teaspoon vanilla extract

2 teaspoons maca powder

CBD oil, dosage according to package directions (optional)

Flaky sea salt, chopped hazelnuts, chopped almonds, chopped pistachios, rose petals, and/or dried fruit, for topping (optional)

In preparation for setting the chocolate, take out a small baking sheet, plate, or container that's around 6 by 6 inches (I use a plastic takeout container). Anything that is roughly this size with a rim or sides will work. Line it with parchment paper.

In a small saucepan, melt the coconut oil over medium heat. Remove from the heat and add the maple syrup, almond butter, cacao powder, vanilla, maca, and CBD (if using). Whisk until smooth and combined.

With a spatula, spoon the chocolate mixture into the prepared vessel and smooth it out until it's about ½ inch thick. Add any desired toppings. Place it into the freezer on a flat surface and freeze for at least 30 minutes, until solid. Use a large knife to cut it into squares, or roughly break it up into pieces with your hands.

Store in an airtight container in the freezer for up to 6 months. Take out a piece anytime you need a divinely chocolatey mood boost.

**customize it**

Try any one of these fun flavor combinations
for toppings:

- Chopped toasted hazelnuts and dried
  cranberries
- Chopped pitted Medjool dates and a
  drizzle of tahini
- Dried rose petals and pistachios
- Almond butter and flaky sea salt
- Crunchy peanut butter and chia seeds
- Granola and toasted coconut flakes

Oh hello there, summer! These pops channel juicy early-summer strawberries and sunshine into one decadent yet refreshing bite. Coconut milk and vanilla make for a creamy base, while antioxidant powerhouses goji berries and strawberries make the whole thing . . . pop! #DontSkipDessert

# strawberry & coconut cream pops

### makes 4 to 8 pops

1 (14-ounce/414ml) can full-fat coconut milk

1 heaping cup strawberries (frozen or fresh), chopped

2 teaspoons goji berries (see page 29)

2 tablespoons maple syrup or raw honey

1 tablespoon vanilla extract

Pinch of salt

3 tablespoons Strawberry Sunshine Chia Compote (page 86) or strawberry jam, for a ripple effect (optional)

In a high-speed blender, combine all the ingredients except the compote. Blend for 40 to 60 seconds, until smooth and combined.

Pour the coconut milk mixture into pop molds. If adding the strawberry compote, spoon about 1 teaspoon into each pop mold and use a pop stick to gently disperse some of the compote and create a swirl effect.

Insert sticks and freeze for at least 5 hours. Run the pop molds under warm water for a few seconds to loosen them up, then remove from the mold. Eat immediately or store the pops in the freezer for up to 3 months.

Sweet tooth? I've got you covered. These fudgy pops will crush your nut-butter cup and ice cream cravings, all while being super good for you too. Coconut milk brings healthy fats to the table, with our beloved raw cacao packing energy and antioxidants.

# chocolate tahini fudgesicles

In a high-speed blender, combine all the ingredients except the garnish. Blend for 40 to 60 seconds, until smooth and combined. Taste and adjust sweetness as desired. Pour the coconut milk mixture into pop molds.

Insert sticks and freeze for at least 5 hours. Run the pop molds under warm water for a few seconds to loosen them up, then remove from the mold.

If you're using the melted chocolate, spread the pops out on a plate or work surface and drizzle with the chocolate. Quickly sprinkle with the coconut flakes (if using) before the chocolate hardens.

Eat immediately or store the pops in the freezer for up to 3 months.

**makes 4 to 8 pops**

1 (14-ounce/414ml) can full-fat coconut milk

2 tablespoons raw cacao powder (see page 27)

¼ cup tahini

2 teaspoons maca powder (optional)

2 to 4 tablespoons maple syrup or raw honey

1 teaspoon vanilla extract

Pinch of salt

Melted chocolate and/or toasted coconut flakes, for garnish (optional)

Good news: these brownies do not taste healthy or gluten-free. They are crispy on top and gooey in the center with a rich dark-chocolate flavor. If that doesn't seal the deal for you, they're also packed with blood-sugar-balancing fiber and protein and mood-boosting raw cacao. Nutty reishi bolsters the antioxidant benefits and blends seamlessly into the decadent batter. Now *that* is a blissful bake.

# boosted sea salt espresso brownies

### makes 12 to 16 brownies

¾ cup coconut oil
(see page 28)

¾ cup raw cacao powder

1¼ cups coconut sugar
or packed brown sugar

1 shot espresso
or 3 tablespoons strongly
brewed coffee

¾ teaspoon salt

1¼ cups semisweet
chocolate chips, divided

1 tablespoon vanilla extract

3 large eggs

1 cup almond flour

¾ teaspoon baking soda

1 tablespoon reishi powder
(optional)

3 tablespoons collagen
powder (optional)

Flaky sea salt, for topping
(optional)

Preheat the oven to 350°F. Line a 10-inch cast-iron skillet or 9 by 9-inch baking pan with parchment paper.

In a medium pot, melt the coconut oil over medium heat.

Off the heat, add the cacao, sugar, espresso, salt, and half of the chocolate chips. Stir well to combine and melt the chocolate chips.

Add the vanilla and eggs and whisk until the mixture is smooth and glossy. Add the almond flour, baking soda, reishi (if using), and collagen (if using), and stir until combined.

Stir in the remaining chocolate chips, reserving 1 to 2 tablespoons for the top. Scrape the batter into the prepared pan. Sprinkle with the reserved chocolate chips.

Bake for 30 to 35 minutes, until the top is slightly crisp and a toothpick inserted into the center is still quite moist. Sprinkle with flaky salt, if using, and set aside to cool for at least 20 minutes (if you can stand it!).

Cool completely and store, tightly wrapped, in the fridge for up to 1 week.

A highlight of my middle school days was meeting up with my girlfriends for rom-com marathons at the local movie theater. If we were feeling spendy, we'd splurge on a bag of butter-lathered popcorn and go to town shaking on the mysterious orange flavoring dust. This grown-up popcorn is just as craveable yet uses smoky spices and nutritional yeast to mimic a nacho-cheese flavor. Prepare to demolish the entire bowl.

# cheezy superfood popcorn

### makes about 7 cups

4 tablespoons ghee or coconut oil, divided

¼ cup popcorn kernels

3 tablespoons nutritional yeast (see page 32), plus more as needed

1 teaspoon ground turmeric, plus more as needed

1 teaspoon garlic salt, plus more as needed

¼ teaspoon chipotle powder, plus more as needed

Salt

In a large pot, warm 1 tablespoon of the ghee over medium heat. When it's hot, add the popcorn kernels. Cover the pot and give it a shake to distribute the kernels evenly.

Cook over medium heat for 3 to 5 minutes, shaking the pot occasionally, until the popping sound slows down to about one pop every few seconds. Remove the pot from the heat. Transfer the popcorn to a large bowl.

In a medium pot, melt the remaining 3 tablespoons ghee. Stir in the nutritional yeast, turmeric, garlic salt, chipotle powder, and salt to taste. Add to the popped corn, stirring with a wooden spoon to evenly distribute the spice mixture (stir, stir, and stir some more). Taste and add more nutritional yeast or spices as desired.

Snack your heart out! Popcorn will stay fresh in an airtight container for 2 to 3 days.

# beauty sleep

Break out your softest pants and furry slippers—
we're getting ready for bed! If you're like me and
savor that last hour before tucking in, you'll love
this section filled with ways to relieve tension,
improve sleep, and revel in your bedtime ritual.

Pre-zzz time is all about slowing down and
soothing the nervous system to prepare it for
rest. As someone who struggled with insomnia
and anxiety for years, I can assure you that these
recipes and tips are treasured, tried, and true.

# how to have a blissful bedtime

There is nothing like the moment of sinking into a soft, fluffy bed at the end of the day. It feels like a hug for your body and soul, a respite from the goings-on of the real world. I know firsthand how bedtime can turn from a pleasure into a frustrating and exhausting experience when you aren't sleeping well. Taking care of our sleep is vital to our overall health—having adequate rest impacts everything from our hunger levels to the inflammation in our bodies to our cognitive function.

Through many years studying how lifestyle and diet impact shut-eye, I have put to the test dozens of things that might make bedtime a more relaxing, restorative experience. I hope these practices inspire a little love for your sleep routine.

## Include sleep-loving foods

Foods consumed during the day affect your quality of sleep. Fill your plate with magnesium-rich leafy greens, nuts, and seeds to reduce adrenaline levels and relax the mind and body. Including unrefined carbohydrates in your diet —whole grains, sweet potatoes, and quinoa—can assist in quality sleep by boosting tryptophan and serotonin, two brain chemicals involved in sleep.

Foods that can prevent a good night's sleep are processed sugars, high-fat foods, and alcohol and caffeine consumed too close to bedtime. If you are snack-ish before bed, a protein- and fiber-rich snack like the Chai Latte Bliss Balls (page 174) could help send you off to dreamland on the right note.

## Create a bedtime ritual

A bedtime ritual may sound a little woo-woo, but even a few minutes of practicing some self-care before bed can have a profound impact over time.

## Drink a soothing tonic

The ritual of making a soothing tonic is a great way to get your body and mindset in the zone for sleep. About 1 to 2 hours before bed, I'll prep my "tonic of the night" to soak up some soothing herbs while reading or watching a movie with my partner. Currently I am loving a tall glass of Tulsi-Lavender Lemonade (page 163) in the evenings.

Herbs that promote rest and relaxation are lavender, chamomile, peppermint, passionflower, valerian, and lemon balm. Some great sleep-promoting adaptogens are reishi, tulsi, and ashwagandha.

## Spa-ify your bathroom

Deck out your tub or shower with a few products that provide a sensory bathing experience. A body scrub promotes circulation while also sloughing off dead skin cells. A bath soak moisturizes your skin while the soothing scents help to calm the mind. Turn washing your face into a mini facial with the help of some cleansers, moisturizers, or face masks. I used to skip my nighttime skincare routine, until I found a cleanser that made my skin feel squeaky clean and a eucalyptus-scented moisturizer that reminded me of a day at the spa.

## Swap screen time for a book

Studies have shown that social media has the most negative impact on sleep when consumed 30 minutes before bed. Instead of getting in some (probably unnecessary) scroll-time before bed, try reading an interesting book. Without the glaring screen and stimulation of your device, you'll likely have an easier time drifting off to sleep.

## Add aromatherapy

Drifting off to the scent of lavender or eucalyptus essential oils wafting out of a diffuser is both luxurious-feeling and an effective tool for a great night's sleep.

## Get comfortable

Set the thermostat to your perfect sleep temperature (optimal temp is between 60° and 67°F), fluff the pillows, spritz a soothing face mist, and slide on a light-blocking eye mask.

## Practice self-massage

The next best thing to a spa treatment before bed? A moisturizing self-massage with lotion. Treat your feet, shoulders, thighs, elbows, and hands—anywhere that needs a little love! I like to choose soothing scents like peppermint, lavender, or rose. Tucking yourself into bed feeling and smelling amazing promotes a feeling of peacefulness.

## Journaling or visualization

Take a few minutes to write down how you are doing, feeling, and staying on top of your goals and aspirations.

Positive visualizations can also help you drift off. Close your eyes and picture yourself living your best life, whatever that looks like to you. Sometimes I will envision my perfect day or my dream vacation or home. I swear it wards off nightmares too!

## Stay consistent

Try to keep your sleep schedule consistent to maintain the timing of your body's internal clock. Your body loves routine and will thank you with better sleep.

This lemonade combines lavender-honey simple syrup with lemon juice, adaptogenic tulsi, and butterfly pea flower powder for antioxidant and zen-inducing benefits. Sip before bed or serve as a mocktail.

# tulsi-lavender lemonade

In a medium saucepan, combine the water, lavender, tulsi, and honey. Bring to a low simmer over medium heat, stirring to dissolve the honey. Stir in the butterfly pea flower powder (if using).

Remove the pan from the heat. Cover and let steep for 30 minutes.

Strain through a fine-mesh sieve into a 1-quart (about 1-liter) jar or pitcher (discard the solids). Add the lemon juice and cold water. Stir to combine, then serve over ice. Sip and luxuriate!

**makes 4 drinks**

1 cup water

1 tablespoon dried culinary lavender or 2 tea bags of lavender tea (see page 31)

1 teaspoon dried tulsi leaves or 1 tea bag of tulsi tea

3 tablespoons raw honey

⅛ teaspoon butterfly pea flower powder, for color (optional)

Juice of 2 lemons

3 cups cold water

Sweet, creamy steamers are simply frothed milk with added flavors or syrups. The "snickerdoodle" component comes from the pleasing combination of maple, cinnamon, and a hint of caramel-like coconut sugar.

# snickerdoodle steamer

In a small saucepan, combine all the ingredients. Cook over medium heat, whisking for 3 to 4 minutes, until warmed through and combined. Froth the mixture using a hand frother or steam wand.

Sip and soak up the cozy.

*Pictured on page 158*

**makes 1 hot drink**

1 cup oat milk

½ teaspoon ground cinnamon

⅛ teaspoon nutmeg

1 to 3 teaspoons coconut sugar or maple syrup

½ teaspoon reishi powder

½ teaspoon vanilla extract

Drink this golden elixir when you're feeling under the weather and enjoy the satisfying bite! Turmeric, ginger, and raw honey are the trifecta of nature's digestive aids and immune supporters, making this an ideal choice for a cozy, nourishing evening tonic. I use a tea bag to make life easier, but feel free to one-up it with fresh turmeric and ginger (see Customize It, below).

# golden turmeric hot toddy

### makes 1 hot toddy

1 tea bag or 1 teaspoon loose-leaf turmeric-ginger tea

1¼ cups boiling water

Juice of ¼ lemon

Pinch of cayenne pepper

1 teaspoon raw honey

To your favorite mug, add the tea bag and pour the boiling water over it. Steep, covered, for at least 5 minutes.

Remove the tea bag (strain if using loose tea or keep it in for a bolder brew). Stir in the lemon juice, cayenne, and honey. Sip and soak up the spicy goodness.

### customize it

Turmeric-ginger tea is widely available in a variety of loose and bagged tea blends at most grocery stores. If you'd prefer a fresh tea option, pour the boiling water over ½ teaspoon each finely grated fresh turmeric and ginger and let it steep.

My passion for mental health and wellness was a large part of the inspiration behind building the tea company Lake & Oak. I turned to healing herbs and foods to manage stress and help tackle some of the insomnia I was experiencing. This dreamy latte is inspired by Ashwagandha + Chill, Lake & Oak's relaxation and sleep tea blend. Naturally sweet and floral chamomile tea is a delicious match for frothed milk, lovely for sipping on as you're winding down for the eve.

# chamomile serenity CBD latte

To your coziest oversized mug, add the tea bag and pour the boiling water over it. Steep, covered, for at least 5 minutes. Remove the tea bag (or strain if using loose tea).

In a small pot, heat the milk over medium heat until hot. Stir in the CBD (if using), honey, and ashwagandha (if using). Froth the milk mixture in the pot using a hand-held milk frother (or see Frothing 101 on page 51 for more frothing methods).

Pour the frothed milk over the steeped tea. Sprinkle with cinnamon if desired. Sip and zen out.

**makes 1 latte**

1 tea bag or 1 heaping teaspoon loose-leaf chamomile tea (any blend with chamomile will work)

¾ cup boiling water

¾ cup plant-based milk

CBD oil, dosage according to package directions (optional; see page 27)

1 teaspoon raw honey

½ teaspoon ashwagandha powder (optional)

Pinch of ground cinnamon (optional)

The golden girl, the Queen Bee, the Beyoncé of all tonics, golden milk is a westernized version of the ancient Indian turmeric-powered drink known as haldi doodh. In the past decade, there have been thousands of recipes and products celebrating golden milk or turmeric lattes as a cure-all golden elixir of health. I can't confirm this golden milk will improve your posture or credit score, but I can say that it is a comforting and delicious cup of golden goodness. The heavy emphasis on sweet cinnamon and complementary spices makes it palatable even to turmeric virgins and the tonic-averse.

# wind-me-down golden mylk

### makes 1 hot drink

1¼ cups plant-based milk

¾ teaspoon ground turmeric

½ teaspoon ground cinnamon

¼ teaspoon ashwagandha powder (see page 26)

Pinch of nutmeg

Pinch of ground ginger

Pinch of freshly ground black pepper

1 teaspoon raw honey

1 teaspoon coconut oil or ghee (optional)

In a medium saucepan, combine all the ingredients. Warm the mixture over medium heat for 3 to 5 minutes, whisking occasionally, until it is hot and a deep yellow color.

For a fluffier version, froth the hot milk directly in the pot with a hand frother, or transfer to a blender and pulse for 10 seconds. Sip and soak up the golden goodness.

When my days are especially stressful, I like to lean on an extra-luxurious bedtime ritual to unwind from the day and prepare for quality sleep. This periwinkle latte feels like self-care in a cup, and the soothing benefits of oat milk and lavender will whisk you away to la-la land. If you don't have dried lavender on hand, you can also use a bagged or loose tea blend that contains lavender.

# blue lavender latte

In a small saucepan, combine the milk, lavender, and butterfly pea flower powder. Heat on low for 6 to 8 minutes, stirring occasionally. Remove the pot from the heat and stir in the honey, vanilla, and CBD if desired.

Strain the mixture through a fine-mesh sieve into your favorite large mug. Sip and chill out.

## makes 1 latte

1¼ cups oat milk or other plant-based milk

1½ teaspoons dried culinary lavender or 1 lavender tea bag (see page 31)

¼ teaspoon butterfly pea flower powder, for color

1 teaspoon Adaptogenic Lavender Honey (page 184) or raw honey

⅓ teaspoon vanilla extract

CBD oil, dosage according to package directions (optional)

---

### ice it, baby
For a refreshing twist, prepare the recipe as directed but serve in a tall glass with plenty of ice.

If you're someone who gets hungry before bed (hands raised) but doesn't want to disturb sleep with something that's difficult to digest, bedtime smoothies might be your thing. Think of it like a healthy milkshake with a balance of fiber, protein, and micronutrients to ease you into bedtime.

# oatmeal cookie smoothie

In a high-speed blender, combine all the ingredients except the granola. Blend for 45 to 60 seconds, until the oats are completely broken down and the mixture is creamy.

Sprinkle with granola (if using) and cinnamon. Slurp and enjoy!

### makes 1 smoothie

1 cup almond milk

2 tablespoons old-fashioned oats (see page 32)

1 cup frozen banana pieces

1 teaspoon almond butter

1 teaspoon vanilla extract

½ teaspoon ground cinnamon, plus more for topping

Pinch of nutmeg

Pinch of ground ginger

Pinch of salt

½ teaspoon ashwagandha powder (optional)

½ cup ice

½ teaspoon raw honey (optional)

Granola, for topping (optional)

Snacking on a few sweet treats before bed is all fun and games until you've consumed enough sugar to keep you up for two extra hours bingeing *Love Is Blind* on Netflix (just me?). These blissful bites are designed to satisfy your nighttime snacking urge without spiking your blood sugar or disturbing your shut-eye. They taste like deliciously spiced doughnuts and pair wonderfully with a nighttime tea. You're going to be obsessed.

# chai latte bliss balls

### makes 10 to 20 bliss balls

2 cups Medjool dates, pitted (see page 32)

1¼ cups raw cashews

¼ cup unsweetened coconut flakes

1 teaspoon ground cinnamon

½ teaspoon ground ginger

¼ teaspoon ground cardamom

½ teaspoon salt

1 teaspoon vanilla extract

1 tablespoon reishi powder (optional)

1 tablespoon maple syrup (optional)

In a small bowl, soak the dates in hot water for 5 minutes, until softened slightly. Drain and set aside.

In a food processor, combine all the ingredients except the dates. Pulse for 45 to 60 seconds, until the mixture becomes fine crumbs. Add the dates. Pulse for another 45 to 60 seconds, until the mixture comes together in a dough-like consistency.

With your hands, form the mixture into 1- to 2-inch balls. Enjoy right away or refrigerate in an airtight container for 2 to 3 weeks. Bliss balls will also keep in the freezer for up to 3 months.

Yes, you can certainly sip tea in the tub, but have you tried steeping *in* your favorite herbs?

If you're a professional bathtubber like me, an herbal bath is a fun and therapeutic way to switch up your typical bubble bath. All you need is a handful of dried herbs and a few drops of essential oil to turn your tub into a mini spa.

# soothing rose bath "tea"

In a large bowl, combine the rose petals, lavender, chamomile, and salt (if using). Add the essential oil and mix with a spoon to combine. Spoon the herb mixture into a bag or satchels (see Customize It, below).

Place the bag in the tub and run a hot bath, allowing the herbs to completely submerge in the water. After steeping for 5 to 6 minutes, gently squeeze the herb bag to encourage extra herb diffusion and benefits.

Inhale, exhale, and soak up the botanical beauty.

### makes 1 herbal bath

2 tablespoons dried rose petals

2 tablespoons dried lavender (see page 31)

2 tablespoons dried chamomile

2 tablespoons coarse Himalayan pink salt (optional)

10 to 15 drops lavender essential oil

### customize it
Keep your bathtub tidy by using a small cotton bag with drawstring closure or a few loose-leaf tea satchels to capture all of the herbs. Alternatively, make your own tea bag by wrapping a layer of cheesecloth around your herbs and tying it at the top with twine. Make sure to leave enough room for water to run through the herbs.

# superfood staples

These go-to staples are on repeat in my tonic kitchen because of their flavor, functionality, and ease of prep.

# salted tahini "caramel"

If you're a fan of savory tahini sauce, this sweet version is going to rock your world. Nutty tahini, maple syrup, and vanilla make a convincing quick caramel sauce for fresh fruit, oatmeal (page 92), ice cream, and yogurt.

### makes about ½ cup

2 tablespoons tahini

2 tablespoons maple syrup

2 tablespoons warm water

¾ teaspoon vanilla extract

¾ teaspoon maca powder
(see page 31)

Pinch of salt

In a medium bowl, combine all the ingredients. Whisk well until the mixture has a creamy sauce consistency. Store in a jar or airtight container in the fridge for up to 7 days.

# sweet sesame ginger dressing

Tangy, spicy, and a punch of umami, this dressing will take your greens, noodles, and grain bowls to a new level. Try it on the Hydrating Spring Roll Salad (page 118) or use it as a marinade for tofu or chicken.

### makes about 1 cup

2 tablespoons tamari or coconut aminos

2 tablespoons chili garlic sauce or sriracha

1 tablespoon toasted sesame oil

2 tablespoons maple syrup

3 tablespoons olive oil

Juice of 1 lime

1 tablespoon raw organic apple cider vinegar
(see page 26)

1 garlic clove, finely grated

1 teaspoon finely grated fresh ginger

½ teaspoon sesame seeds
(optional)

To a small jar, add all the ingredients and shake well to combine. Store, refrigerated, for up to 1 week.

# dreamy coconut whipped cream

Do you love that glorious feeling of spraying whipped cream directly into your mouth? This coconut whipped cream is even better—best enjoyed by the spoon while standing in front of the fridge. I first tried coconut whipped cream when I worked at Bunner's Bakeshop, Toronto's cult-favorite vegan bakery. We made super-sized batches of it and squirted them into the centers of chocolate cupcakes. One day I will re-create that epic cupcake, but in the meantime, there is this delicious coconut cream to throw on top of your cozy beverages and desserts. Whip it, baby!

Chill the cans of coconut milk in the refrigerator overnight or in the freezer for 1½ hours (no longer than that, or it will be difficult to work with).

Open the cans and use a spoon or spatula to remove the thickened coconut milk on the top, transferring it to a large metal mixing bowl. Discard the coconut water, or reserve it to use later (it's great in smoothies).

Using an electric mixer, beat the coconut milk on high speed for 20 to 30 seconds, until creamy. Add the maple syrup and vanilla. Beat for 60 to 90 seconds, until fluffy and whipped. Do not over-whip. Taste and add more sweetener or vanilla as needed.

Use immediately, or cover and refrigerate. The coconut whipped cream will set the longer it chills. It will keep in the fridge for up to 5 days or in the freezer for up to 6 months. No need to re-whip before serving.

### makes about 1½ cups

3 (14-ounce/414ml) cans full-fat coconut milk (Thai Kitchen brand works very well)

2 tablespoons maple syrup or coconut sugar, plus more as needed

1 teaspoon vanilla extract, plus more as needed

### switch it up

This luscious cream can be used in a variety of desserts and tonics, from hot chocolate and lattes to pies and plant-forward desserts. Play around with flavors and try adding cacao powder for a chocolate whip, or ground cinnamon and nutmeg for a pleasantly spiced version.

# easy chai tea concentrate

Have you ever wondered why your café-bought chai tea latte tastes so great, but homemade chai is so lackluster? That's probably thanks to chai tea concentrate, a sugar-heavy syrup often packed with artificial ingredients and preservatives. This recipe cuts the fluff so you can make your own life-changing chai syrup at home, using real tea and nature's superfood, honey. I like to make a batch on a Sunday morning and steam up perfectly spiced chai lattes all week.

In a small pot, bring the water to a boil. Add the tea and reduce the heat to a very low simmer. Simmer for 25 minutes, until the liquid is reduced by one-quarter.

Stir in the honey and vanilla. Remove the tea bags or strain the tea and let cool. Refrigerate in a lidded jar or airtight container for up to 3 weeks.

### makes about 3 cups

4 cups water

10 of your favorite chai tea bags or 10 teaspoons loose-leaf chai tea

¼ cup raw honey

1 tablespoon vanilla extract

### switch it up

To turn this syrup into a delicious latte, just mix 1 part frothed milk (see page 51) with 1 part warmed chai concentrate. For an iced version, pour everything directly into a glass and top with ice.

# adaptogenic lavender honey

Infusing your favorite superfoods or adaptogens into raw honey is a fun way to customize the flavor and power up the benefits. This lavender honey is a juicy burst of floral flavor, and the stress-relieving benefits of lavender and ashwagandha don't hurt either. I like to drizzle it in my evening tea latte or enjoy a spoonful as a sweet treat.

## makes 1 cup

1 cup raw honey

1 tablespoon dried culinary lavender (see page 31)

1½ teaspoon ashwagandha powder (optional)

In a medium pot, combine all the ingredients. Heat over low heat for 2 to 4 minutes, stirring to combine, until warmed slightly (do not let the mixture boil). Transfer to a jar and let sit at room temperature for at least 24 hours.

Use a fine-mesh sieve to strain out the lavender. Store the honey in a lidded jar or airtight container in a cool, dry place for up to 6 months.

### customize it

With the same method, you can use different superfoods to create custom honey to your personal taste. Rose petals, cacao, ground cinnamon, and ground turmeric are a few of my other favorite mix-ins.

# closing gratitude

Thank you, dear reader, for picking up this book and allowing me to be a small part of your rituals in wellness and self-care. I am extremely grateful to be able to share some of my most treasured practices, recipes, and tools for well-being with you. I can't wait to see what tips and tonics you try!

The amazing Lake & Oak community: Thank you for kindness, generosity, and endless excitement for all things tea. I am constantly inspired by you, and it's a blessing to connect with so many of you through your daily tea practice. I revel in every photo, comment, review, and piece of feedback you share with us.

My *Super Tonics* team: Thank you for believing in this project and sharing your infectious excitement and curiosity about tonics with me.

The Ten Speed Press and Appetite by Random House teams: It's beyond an honor to be represented by you and work with some of the brilliant minds behind some of my favorite books that I have dog-eared throughout the years. Dervla Kelly, Kim Keller, Rachel Brown, Terry Deal, Emma Campion, Zoey Brandt, and Nicole Sarry— thank you for sharing your inspiration and wisdom to make this book the best it can be. Learning from you and working with you has been life-changing.

Carly Watters: Thank you for taking a chance on this tea business owner and recipe developer with a big dream to share her passion for superfoods with the world. I will never forget the happy dance after our first phone call. Cheers to many more of those.

Jocelynne Flor: Your incredible vision and photography style has inspired me for years, and this book (and Lake & Oak Tea Co.) would not be the same without your beautiful work, which helps tell our story. Your passion for wellness and self-care shines through in everything you create. I hope to make many more beautiful things together.

Jules Lee: I'm so appreciative that your incredible talent could be a part of this book. You constantly amaze me with your work, and I have never felt more confident in front of a camera thanks to you. Thank you for being a part of the Lake & Oak team.

My husband and partner, Peter: Thank you for inspiring in me a gritty persistence and resilience that wasn't there before. You remind me to enjoy life through all of the ups and downs, and you can cut the stress of a day with your (questionable) humor. Thank you for bearing the burden of being "the tidy one" and doing your best to ignore the stains, splats, and splatters that result from a day of tonic-testing.

Mom and Dad: Thank you for encouraging my early cooking efforts and always having something kind to say about my food (before my ego could stand to take a hit). Making people happy through food is one of my favorite parts of life and I have learned that through cooking for you. You instilled a passion for reading and writing in me at a young age, and through all of life's adventures I feel lucky to be able to express myself through writing. Thank you for rolling up your sleeves and getting your hands covered in beet powder and turmeric to help spread superfood teas and good cheer—you make Lake & Oak Tea Co. feel like home.

My sister, Sarah: You will always be the cooler, more creative sister I look up to. Thanks for being there to talk tonics, mental health, self-care, and wild wellness trends with me. I love you.

My girlfriends: Thanks for loving me throughout the years in all my shapes, sizes, lifestyles, passions, interests, and mental states. You are incredible, inspiring women. I look up to you, and you help me feel happy to be me.

My colleagues, past and present: Every one of you has left an impression on my life and cooking style, and I am so grateful to those who have helped me learn or simply shared the joy of food with me. The inspired teams at B.Love, Bunner's, Chef's Plate, Hello Fresh, and my current superstars at Lake & Oak, in particular, have left their mark.

# index

Published in the United States by Ten Speed Press, an imprint of Random House,
a division of Penguin Random House LLC, New York.
TenSpeed.com
RandomHouseBooks.com

Ten Speed Press and the Ten Speed Press colophon are registered trademarks
of Penguin Random House LLC.

Simultaneously published in Canada by Appetite by Random House®,
a division of Penguin Random House Canada Limited.

Photographs on pages 8, 18, 25, 39, 94, and 126 by Jules Lee.
Typefaces: Letter Omega's Grafical, Latinotype's Recoleta, and Set Sail Studios' Better Times

Library of Congress Cataloging-in-Publication Data
Names: Youngson, Meredith, author.
Title: Super tonics : 75 adaptogen-packed recipes to boost immunity, sleep, beauty,
    and wellness / by Meredith Youngson.
Description: First edition. | California : Ten Speed Press, [2023]
Identifiers: LCCN 2022024976 (print) | LCCN 2022024977 (ebook)
    ISBN 9781984861672 (trade paperback) | ISBN 9781984861689 (ebook)
Subjects: LCSH: Blenders (Cooking) | Smoothies (Beverages) | Fruit juices.
    Nutrition. | Health. | LCGFT: Cookbooks.
Classification: LCC TX840.B5 .Y68 2023 (print) | LCC TX840.B5 (ebook)
    DDC 641.5/893—dc23/eng/20220809
LC record available at https://lccn.loc.gov/2022024976
LC ebook record available at https://lccn.loc.gov/2022024977

Trade Paperback ISBN: 978-1-9848-6167-2
eBook ISBN: 978-1-9848-6168-9

Printed in China

Acquiring editors: Dervla Kelly and Rachel Brown | Editors: Kim Keller and Rachel Brown
Production editor: Terry Deal
Designer: Nicole Sarry | Art director: Emma Campion | Production designer: Mari Gill
Photographers: Jocelynne Flor (food) and Jules Lee (lifestyle)
Production manager: Jane Chinn | Prepress color manager: Nick Patton
Copyeditor: Carey Jones | Proofreaders: Kathy Brock and Rachel Markowitz |
Indexer: Ken DellaPenta
Publicist: Natalie Yera | Marketer: Andrea Portanova

10 9 8 7 6 5 4 3 2 1

First Edition